Celebrating Life On Our Own Terms

Dr Angela C. Robertson

Celebrating Life On Our Own Terms

Paradise Publishing 2020

ISBN: 978-0-473-51912-4 Paperback
ISBN: 978-0-473-51914-8 Kindle
ISBN: 978-0-473-51913-1 Epub

Cover Image:
Steven Novak Novakillustrations.com

By the same author

Life On Our Own Terms
The first collection of stories in the **'Older and Bolder'** series

Available online or from your favourite bookstores
ISBN: 978-0-473-50082-5 Paperback
ISBN: 978-0-473-50084-9 Kindle
ISBN: 978-0-473-50083-2 Epub

CONTENTS

"It is not the years in your life, but the life in your years that counts"
Adlai Stevenson

PREFACE

I wrote this book because I was interested in the stage of life where it is possible to look both back and forward. It is a very thought-provoking and empowering experience and helps to clarify who we are and what's important in our lives. A huge debt of gratitude is due to the men and women featured in this book who generously shared their stories with me. In their 50's, 60's, 70's and 80's, they are mindfully aware of their personal life experience and the people they have met along the way that have influenced who they are today.

These individuals are from all walks of life. Age is irrelevant to them. They appreciate that life is a gift for us to enjoy so they make conscious choices about how they spend their time and who they spend their time with. They actively channel their energy into purposeful meaningful activities. They pursue their passions, proactively maintain their health and wellbeing, invest in meaningful relationships, enjoy a good laugh, seek new opportunities and challenges, engage in productive work whether paid or unpaid, and are connected to the community. As they age, these individuals are not chasing lost youth. On the contrary, they look forward to expanding their horizons by creating and making the most of the opportunities the future brings.

It's a privilege to be able to share these stories with you. Later life offers new possibilities for personal growth and the opportunity to fulfil long-nurtured ambitions. These individuals are celebrating life on their own terms and, inspired by their example, whatever our age and circumstances, so can we!

"Your story is the greatest legacy that you will leave to your friends. It's the longest-lasting legacy you will leave to your heirs"
Steve Saint

INTRODUCTION

Globally, the population is ageing. By 2025 there will be an estimated 1.25 billion people over the age of 60, increasing to an incredible 2 billion by 2050. Centenarians, semi-centenarians (people aged 105-109 years) and super-centenarians (those aged 110 and over) are growing in numbers. Although there is no way of knowing how long we are going to live, with dramatic improvements in health care and notable increases in life expectancy, there is a good chance that many of us will live to 90 and beyond – a lot longer than our predecessors. So, it makes sense to embrace the ageing process, take good care of ourselves, enjoy life's pleasures and make the most of the opportunities later life presents.

Ageing is inevitable. The diversity within the older population, given the breadth of chronological age in decades, experience, talent, capability, interests, personal circumstances, gender and ethnicity is incredible. Our older population is in fact an intergenerational community. Whilst it is acknowledged that people age differently and have different aspirations and needs, age brings advantages that no previous generation has had. This is a cause for celebration as the potential to live longer and healthier lives creates new opportunities and exciting challenges for everyone. Despite this news, many of us struggle with the reality of growing older. For some unfathomable reason few of us look forward to being 50, 60, 70, 80 or 90 years of age. Looking ahead, towards what we may traditionally call 'retirement', we have potentially only lived for two-thirds of our lives. Compulsory retirement is a thing of the past in the developed world. A new life-stage has been created for which we have no terminology. We are growing older, but we are not 'over the hill', 'worn out', 'un-productive', 'old' or 'elderly' at any pre-determined age. For many the 'old age pensioner' label is out-of-date and the terms 'seniors', 'senior citizen' and 'elder' seem irrelevant to some folk given the diversity of the population in the second half of life.

It's not unusual for adults, regardless of their chronological age, to say they don't feel their age. Many individuals believe age is a state of mind. After all, one's age is just a number. While it is appreciated that we are all wired differently, how we age and how we feel about it influences our lifestyle choices. The chances of living a full, healthy enjoyable life are higher than ever when we make good lifestyle choices to maximise the benefits and minimise the drawbacks of getting older. For many, mid-life is a time for reflection. It's a phase in our lives when we take stock of what we've experienced to date – what we've achieved, and what and who is important in our lives. We become mindfully aware of what has gone before and more mindful about the present and the future. The second half of life is an opportunity to re-vision and re-ignite our lives. We can change gears if we choose to. We can refocus our time and energy on things that matter most, spend time with the people we care about and consciously celebrate life on our own terms. This phase of life has the potential to be even more fulfilling that what has gone before, depending on one's mindset.

What thoughts come to mind when you think ahead? On the same journey myself I wondered how others had approached this stage in their lives. What was their perspective on ageing? Had they planned 'retirement'? How did they transition from one stage of life to another or was this a continuous journey? How were they spending their additional years? Like many people I read widely on the subject, but I wanted to hear personal stories from ordinary, everyday people, who were also on this life journey. I randomly asked people in New Zealand to share their stories with me and where possible did this in exchange for a pot of home-made jam. During our conversations I captured the context of their earlier lives, their plans and lifestyle choices. It was a humbling experience and so began what was to become the collection of cameo stories that feature in the Older and Bolder series of books. These individuals are living fabulous, fulfilling lives on their own terms and it's with their permission that I can share their stories with you.

Let me introduce you to them.

KIRSTY GREEN

Kirsty grew up in Wellington. Looking back, she said she has always been interested in baking. She recalls making lots of banana and Christmas cakes with her neighbour, which was always a fun experience and she was good at it. Kirsty said she always wanted to cook and enjoyed scanning cookery books and magazines; the Australian Woman's Weekly Dinner Party Cookbook played a huge role in creating exotic family dinners.

On leaving school, after a few months of 7th form, it's not surprising that she was attracted to the hospitality industry, securing her first job in a café in the Harbour City Centre (the old DIC) in Wellington. It was here that she had the chance to get practical experience in the hospitality trade. Encouraged by a woman she worked with she became interested in Cordon Bleu cooking. When she saw an opportunity to train at the Cordon Bleu Training School in Parnell, Auckland she took the plunge and registered to attend the three-month course. Kirsty, who at the time was 18 years old, resigned from her job and relocated to Auckland where she rented a room from her brother who was living there at the time.

Kirsty really enjoyed the intensive Cordon Bleu training course, which she describes as being very 'hands-on'. Every morning was spent preparing and cooking what was on the menu that day for lunch, and the afternoons were dedicated to learning the theory. When she finished her training, Kirsty returned to her hometown and went to work at the Parsons Nose Café in Khandallah. She worked there on and off for about 10 years and there was always a job there when she needed one. Kirsty loved working in the hospitality industry, especially in the suburbs, and knew that one day she would buy and manage her own café.

Sometime later she met Rebecca, a friend of a friend, who owned a café called Kalamata, in Karori. Kirsty and Rebecca worked well together and over a two-year period the café had built a solid reputation and was popular with their rapidly expanding customer base. Kirsty said she learned a lot in the time she worked with Rebecca. When the café came up for sale, she seized the opportunity to make her dream of owning her own café a reality, bought it, became her own boss and made the transition into managing people. Kirsty owned and managed Kalamata café for eight years and with the support of 'great staff' during this period, the business was not only enjoyable, but extremely successful.

As the years passed, Kirsty was ready to move on. She looked into buying a building in Thorndon with a little café and two apartments and lined up the cash but got distracted by the thought of a converted container bach (small holiday cottage). She found herself at Te Horo, a small seaside community 77 kilometres north of Wellington, to look at a section. Te Horo Beach is situated off the State Highway between Peka Peka and Waikanae to the south, and Otaki to the north. There was an open home around the corner. Kirsty recalls how she felt when she looked at a property located at 50 Dixie Street, just one street back from the beach and knew 'it felt so right – I belong here'. Two days later she made the decision to make a lifestyle change and bought the property. As Kirsty still owned and operated the Kalamata café she lived in her home in Wellington during the week and spent the weekends in Te Horo. She travelled back and forth each week until she sold Kalamata four years later, and then worked two days a week for Kelda and Paul at Nikau at the City Art Gallery in the bakery. While there, she discovered a huge blue bus on Trade Me. She visited it in New Plymouth, and on her way home, decided to buy it and so the adventure began.

When she finally moved up to Te Horo, Kirsty worked for Ruth Pretty Catering and Cooking School on a casual basis for the next 12 months, while going through the process of opening up the bus in the front garden of her little house in Dixie Street. The bus, originally known as the 'Rolling Roadhouse Café', was fitted with a gas oven, but needed to be wired so she could install the coffee machine and pop in a fridge or two, and plumbed up so she could have running water. Reflecting on this journey Kirsty said there were many ups and downs. As the inspiration for the café was not a traditional 'run of the mill' experience for some people, it was challenging for people in authority to visualise the possibilities. As a result, the whole process took quite some time to set up. It took a good 18 months to get the consents and the bus ready for trade. Nevertheless, her patience, resolve, experience and reputation paid off when the little quirky Bus Stop Café in the small seaside community became a huge success attracting people from all over the district.

After two years of trading in Dixie Street, the business became just too big for the front garden, so Kirsty had to close. Kirsty erected a big sign at her Dixie Street address saying 'Thank you' to her customers for the patronage and closed the Bus Stop café. The bus remained in the garden and Kirsty bought a share of a little art gallery called Blue Skies at Hyde Park in Te Horo. When this closed, she joined the Artists and Crafters at Artscape and returned to Ruth Pretty's on a casual basis. After a year or so, the opportunity arose to buy 10 acres on Sims Road, just one kilometre away from Dixie Street. Kirsty convinced her mother that she'd love to go halves on the property, so they did. Their tender was accepted and so began a new phase in Kirsty and her Mum's life journey.

Kirsty initially rented out her Dixie Street house, while she and her Mum moved into their new home in Sims Road. Although the bus had not been driven for six years, Kirsty's friend Brent borrowed some batteries, added some diesel and it started first pop. Once again Kirsty applied for the appropriate resource consents to re-establish her café at her new address.

While waiting for this process to be completed, and with the help of good friends she cleared some of the section, without losing its unique rustic charm, installed the bakehouse next to the bus, erected a building and a tent to house tables and chairs for her customers and installed a toilet block. For visitors, the whole experience is welcoming and pet friendly with a huge garden where children can play safely.

Kirsty Green at Bus Stop

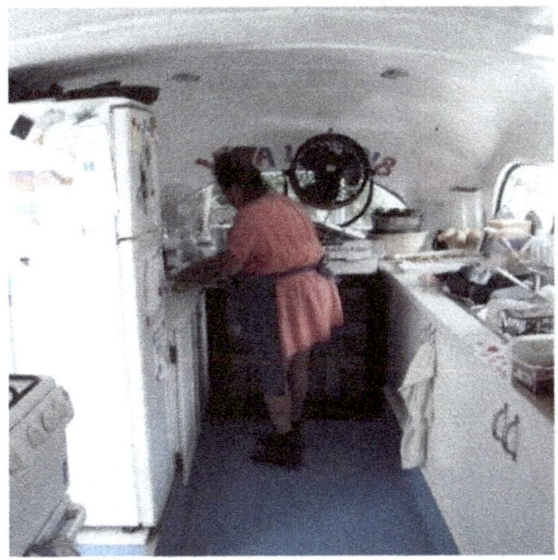

Inside the bus

The buildings have been purposefully designed and built with recycled materials, are visually, artistically appealing and include a little shop selling produce and crafts. Kirsty uses biodegradable plates and all the cups and wooden cutlery are recycled by friends Julie and Heather, who pot seedlings to sell in the paper cups and use the cutlery as plant labels. A fridge freezer, painted bright blue, has been recycled and strategically placed in the garden as a community book and DVD exchange.

In the second year Kirsty built a sunroom, installed braziers and provided both indoor and outdoor seating made from recycled scrap metal.

Ten macrocarpa trees were taken down to make space for the operation and enable more light into the seating area. Accordingly, a lot of firewood was accumulated so several artistic Norwegian wood piles were erected adding character to the grounds. The café, which is hugely successful, is open every weekend, Friday-Sunday 9am-4pm.

Kirsty's reputation and the venue attracts not only local people including horse-riders, cyclists, pedestrians, and community groups, but people from all over the place including day trippers from Wellington.

Reflecting on the journey Kirsty said, "if you enjoy what you do it's not work". She is intuitive and says, "I don't think about things too much". She tends to trust her instincts believing there are 'no wrong decisions' although there are times, she admits, when she could have made better ones. Kirsty's philosophy is not to talk about things for too long before making it (the idea) happen. She said, "if it feels right then I'll do it' and 'will work with the process", whatever that may be and no matter how long it takes. Kirsty, who is in her early 50's, makes conscious choices and doesn't intend to live in fear. As she says she would rather "take the power back and enjoy life and do what I want to do" regardless of the naysayers. Her motto is 'just do it' as she believes you evolve and adapt as you go. Kirsty and her Mum intend to do just that into the foreseeable future.

You can find out more information about Kirsty and the Bus Stop Café on her Facebook Page

www.facebook.com/pages/Bus-Stop-Café/1923797187907035

Bus Stop also has excellent reviews on Trip Advisor.

TODD ZANER

Todd, an only child, was born in Hollywood, in Southern California. His parents, Leon and Lucille Zaner, who were originally from New York, had lived in Los Angeles for about 10 years before Todd was born. The story goes that Todd was born following his parents' 'second honeymoon' cruise in the Mediterranean, where they were celebrating their 10th wedding anniversary. While they were on the cruise, Todd's parents had become friendly with one of the ship's mates Peter Dixon from Wellington, New Zealand. After the holiday, Todd's parents and Peter corresponded regularly with each other for many years.

Todd's father, who was a psychologist, was employed as a Vocational Guidance Counsellor with the Los Angeles school system, but unfortunately, he lost his job when the organisation downsized. Incredibly, the five Counsellors involved literally drew straws to see who would get the two remaining jobs in their field. When Todd's father drew one of the short straws, he became unemployed. The family made the decision to leave the bustle of Los Angeles and move to New Zealand for a complete change of lifestyle. Todd was eight years old when they moved to Wellington where the family stayed with their old friend, the Second Mate, until they were able to get their own home. Todd attended Wilton School, (now known as Otari School), and as a teenager went to high school at Onslow College, in Johnsonville.

Growing up Todd had a passion for radio. It had always intrigued him, and he dreamt about being 'on air'. One of his new 'kiwi' friends had given him a radio, which he spent hours listening to. He really enjoyed all aspects of what was broadcasted – continuity (announcements, messages, programme schedules and descriptions of forthcoming programmes) and of course the music. He particularly enjoyed the quiz shows on 2ZB where listeners were given a descriptive clue and then asked, 'What am I – an animal, vegetable or mineral?' and were encouraged to ring the radio station with the answer. Todd loved these quizzes and actively participated whenever he could. Fortuitously, Todd had a friend whose father worked at 'Broadcasting House' in Wellington, which, in its heyday, used to be home for several different radio stations. The boys, who were both interested in radio, were given the opportunity to have a look around the studios and could play around after hours. Todd recalls it being a real treat and great fun!

In 1980, aged 17, Todd finished school and went to work for National Mutual Insurance Company. He was still very enthusiastic about radio and, as a passionate listener, took note of how the news readers and announcers spoke and the quality and tone of their voice. He decided that he would need to invest in speech and voice training if he was going to realise this dream and work in radio. Todd took lessons with Hewitt Humphrey, Radio New Zealand's National Presenter who seemed to speak with a plum in his mouth. The lessons were 'really helpful'. In 1983, to gain experience in the field, Todd began doing voluntary work for Wellington Access Radio, and 'Radio Active' Victoria University's radio station. Over the next three years Todd worked on a diverse range of radio programmes including a mix of live and pre-recorded music programmes, alternative programmes on the weekends, continuity hosting, reading weather forecasts, community news items etc. He also learned how to manage the technical side of radio broadcasting as well as managing specific radio shows. His voluntary work – where his passion lay, was all in addition to his 'day job' at the Insurance Company.

In 1985, quite by chance Todd heard an advertisement inviting people to join a 'Broadcasting Development Programme' with Radio Windy. It was an eight-week self-funded 'hands-on' block course where students would learn copywriting, radio announcement and the specifics of radio broadcasting. Three hundred people applied to do this course, from which 30 applicants were selected. Todd was one of the lucky ones. Five months later he secured his first paid radio role working the graveyard shift – midnight to 6am over the Christmas/New Year period with Radio Windy. As this wasn't a permanent role, he continued juggling both jobs, the radio station at night, and the insurance company role during the day.

Following a trip overseas in 1986, Todd was offered weekend paid work with Radio Windy. For the next four years he worked weekends and undertook on-call work for the radio station in parallel to his work at National Mutual. During this period, he attended a 'Radio Personality' training course with Lindsay Yeo – a well know radio identity in New Zealand. For many years Lindsay was the host for the Breakfast Show for the Wellington radio station 2ZB. It was a fantastic opportunity to learn from and work with this radio icon.

Todd graduated from the course with a Diploma. Todd regarded Lindsay as his mentor and modelled his own radio style on Lindsay's and, as such, has remained in contact with Lindsay ever since.

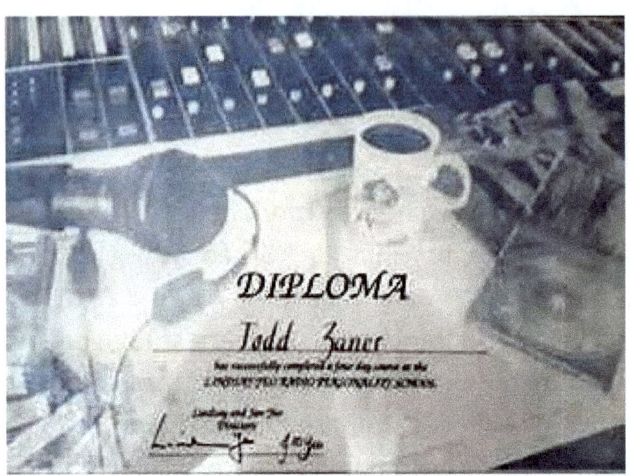

In 1990, there was a recession and National Mutual downsized their business in New Zealand. After serving 10 years with the company Todd was made redundant. This life event triggered Todd to look further afield and through his contacts he secured his first full-time radio job in Tauranga with Radio Bay of Plenty. His 'on-air' slot was the early evening show 5-9pm Monday-Friday each week, where he facilitated continuity, music and kept the public up to date with the news and the weather. Fifteen months later he transferred to Masterton to become the programme director and host the breakfast show for Radio Wairapapa. Todd enjoyed this role for six years. Regrettably, a restructure took place late 1997, and he was made redundant for the second time in his life.

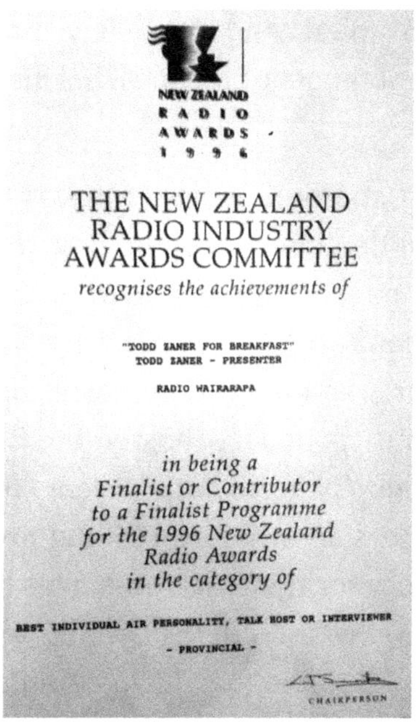

Over the years Todd gained a great deal of experience in broadcasting. He was known in the industry, understood the culture, was skilled as a radio presenter, programme director and he was familiar with the technical equipment – in effect he was an 'all-rounder' in the trade. Within a month of being made redundant he was approached by the manager of the opposition who owned two private radio stations – one located in Masterton and the other in Paraparaumu; 2XX. Todd was offered the Breakfast Show in Paraparaumu, called 'Magic 1377'. Traditionally the Breakfast Show is 'on-air' between 6-9am each day offering listeners a cheerful, upbeat start to their day. Todd's music selection usually comprised the Top 40 which appeals to listeners during breakfast hours. Within a year the two radio stations were merged as one and Todd became the overall Breakfast Show host operating on both the am and fm radio channels. He loved working in the purpose-built studio and over a five-year period he had the opportunity to meet and interview politicians, famous musicians and members of the local business community.

A private radio station, 'Beach FM' was also operating in Paraparaumu at the time. When Johnny Douglas, Beach FM's Programme Manager retired, Todd switched stations to take on this operational role. As Programme Manager he was responsible for recruiting and rostering the staff and selecting the music, and later hosted the Breakfast Show for Beach FM as well. Over the next 13 years there were several changes in ownership at Beach FM and unfortunately Todd faced redundancy for the third time in his life in 2016. Todd had literally travelled around the country working for various stations. After all, radio was his passion, his life. This life event was a significant blow.

Another radio station, 'Coastal Access Radio' operated from Waikanae with a very small staff of three. This station is one of 12 radio stations around the country that are publicly funded by 'New Zealand on Air'. The manager of this station, Graeme Joyes, knew Todd. Graeme suggested Todd could undertake voluntary work at this station while he considered his long-term employment options. Todd accepted the opportunity and offered to initiate and host a Breakfast Show for Coastal Access Radio, a show the station had never had before. The proposal was accepted and 18 months later, when a paid staff member retired, Todd was offered the Programme Manager's position. Todd has worked for Coastal Access Radio ever since and considers the crew that works there, which comprises close to 50 volunteers, to be like family to him. The station's ethos is community focused, which is important to Todd and he gets to utilise all of his skills and experience, - programme management, broadcasting and technical skills. On reflection Todd said his career 'has come full circle' from where he started in radio all those years ago. He is incredibly grateful to have worked with amazing people along the way, many of whom like him, were just starting out on their career and then shot to fame. Hilary Pankhurst – now Hilary Barry was a news editor and his co-host in Masterton in the early 1990's when she was just starting out herself. Hilary is now a highly regarded journalist and television personality in New Zealand with a distinguished career.

Todd at work

Although Todd regards himself as a shy private person, he has always followed his passion, remained focused on his goal, been prepared to learn, and despite being thrown many curve balls, pushed on in his trade. He considers one of the major lessons he learned on his journey through life is to be flexible in his approach to what he wanted to do. He is happy to work for a smaller radio station as he is a 'Jack of all Trades' in broadcasting. He is always willing to help others in the craft volunteering to help plan the programmes, select the music, facilitate the quizzes, write the commercials, interview the guests and edit the recordings and manage the technical equipment. Todd's career in broadcasting spans almost 40 years, during which time he has maintained strong connections with his colleagues in the field and is frequently asked to be a guest speaker for various clubs and events.

Todd's radio studio

Now in his late 50's, Todd enjoys time with his two adult children and his granddaughter, and visits to extended family overseas. He appreciates his life has had its ups and downs but remains passionate about his craft. He has no plans to retire. Looking ahead he says he 'will always be part of the broadcasting industry'. He loves what he does and is very connected to the community in which he lives and works. A life member of Kapiti Old Boys Cricket Club, he plays cricket in his spare time, enjoys spectator sport and is an active member of local quiz teams. If you are looking for a speaker Todd can be contacted via Facebook or on email todd@coastaccessradio.org.nz

"If you are passionate about it, pursue it, no matter what anyone else thinks. That's how dreams are achieved" –
Unknown

PAULA RICHARDSON

Paula, who was born in Scotland, emigrated to New Zealand with her family when she was four years old. The family initially settled in Nelson and later moved to a lifestyle block in Wanganui in the North Island. Paula's father had a farming background. He was used to growing vegetables and caring for animals, and the semi-rural environment was perfect for the family who enjoyed the outdoor life that included bush walks and tramping in the hills. Paula and her brother went to school in Wanganui. Like many children Paula enjoyed school, especially the sciences and regularly played hockey as a teenager.

When Paula left school, she followed her passion with science and moved to Upper Hutt to study Pharmacy at the Central Institute of Technology. While studying she met Graeme, an engineering student, who shared Paula's love of the outdoors. When Paula graduated, she and Graeme got married and moved to Christchurch in the South Island so that Graeme could attend University to finish his engineering degree. In those days it was easy for Paula to get work as a Pharmacist. While they were in the South Island, the couple worked hard all week and enjoyed camping, tramping and skiing at Mount Hutt in their free time. When Graeme graduated, he secured a job in Napier, so the couple returned to the North Island where they started a family. When their two children were little, Paula worked as a Pharmacist after hours so she could spend time with them during the day.

A new job opportunity for Graeme brought the family to Wellington where the couple bought a home in Tawa. As Paula wasn't known in the district, she made the decision to buy her own business and bought a pharmacy in Porirua which was close to home. She loved owning her own business in the multicultural community that the pharmacy served. Reflecting on the experience Paula said she wasn't known in the area, but the locals were very open and accepting of her and her children, who often helped her in the shop, and the family soon became part of the fabric of the community. Paula, who is a people-centred person, enjoyed creating a pleasant, friendly environment for her staff, recognising that people spend more time at work than they do at home. In her words 'Pharmacy is a worthwhile and responsible job and great job for people who like people'. Paula also enjoyed providing work experience for students and interns. She saw it as an opportunity for the young people to get practical work experience, while at the same time she and her staff had the chance to learn from the younger generation, who were also familiar with the latest technology in their industry.

While the children were growing up the family enjoyed skiing trips to Mount Hutt, Wanaka, Ruapehu and regularly went biking and tramping. The children also shared Paula's interest in hockey. While living in Tawa, a Canadian and a Swedish family, who also lived in the neighbourhood, introduced the family to 'inline-hockey' – a sport that is similar to ice-hockey. This is a fast-paced competitive game, played on a hard surface. Inline hockey teams wear comparable kit to ice hockey teams, except they use inline skates instead of ice skates. Paula and the children were captivated with the sport, which at the time, was relatively new to New Zealand and thought it would be fun to establish an adult and a children's team in the district. Paula and the children became members of the 'Tawa Typhoons' team. Over time she helped form a Seniors, a Womens and a Masters team.   The family, in their respective teams competed with clubs in Wanganui, Palmerston North, Levin, Kapiti, the Hutt Valley and Wellington. The New Zealand Hockey Association was formed in 1995 and is affiliated to the New Zealand Ice Hockey Association. National Club Championships commenced in 1996, and Regional Championships commenced in 1997. Senior World Championships are held annually, with New Zealand first qualifying for a place in the Asia/Pacific Qualification Tournament in 1999. The family had great fun pursuing this sport and made some good friendships with other families who shared their love of the game.

When the children grew up and left home, Paula and Graeme made the decision to relocate to the Kapiti Coast. They sold their family home in Tawa and purchased a three-and-a-half-acre lifestyle block eleven years ago. Here they have plenty of room to grow their own vegetables, and raise their chickens, sheep and pigs. They are also beekeepers and enjoy the established native trees on the property. Three years ago, their son Mike and his wife Hannah, who had just got married, bought a lifestyle block in the same street. Now the couple have a daughter Lily who is one-year old. Paula says it's great to be so close to the family. When another lifestyle block became available in the same street, Paula encouraged her parents to think about relocating to Kapiti themselves. This was a major decision for them as they had lived in Wanganui for more than 40 years. The proximity to the family, the connectedness to the community and retention of the semi-rural lifestyle swayed their decision to make the move. Now each of the families can retain their independence, while at the same time strengthen their connectedness, socialise together when they want to and can support each other when required, without having to travel long distances.

Following the move to Kapiti, Paula commuted backwards and forwards to Porirua to work in her Pharmacy for the next ten years. One day, she realised she didn't want the responsibility for the business anymore. Although she loved her work, she wanted to slow down and spend more time on some of the other things in life she enjoyed doing. In her 50's, after 25 years in business, she sold her Pharmacy.

Paula on her last day of work at her pharmacy

Reflecting on her decision, she said she knew it was the right time and therefore the decision was easy to make. Paula has no regrets and hadn't lost her passion for people and pharmacy. She now works part-time 2-3 days a week at a local pharmacy. Paula said she really likes the job, feels she is doing worthwhile work, takes the responsibility seriously and intends to stay in the role for as long as she is enjoying it.

Now that she has more free time Paula has the flexibility to visit her daughter and grandchildren in Brisbane when she wants to.

Paula and her grandchildren

As a member of a local Tramping Club she goes on day and weekend hikes. Both she, and her husband enjoy biking long distances. One of the tracks they have completed is the 70-kilometre Queen Charlotte cycle trail in the Marlborough Sounds - one of New Zealand's best single-track mountain bike rides, and the longest piece of continuous single track in the country.

Paula and Graeme tramping in New Zealand

Paula and Graeme also enjoy intrepid journeys – walking and biking. They have biked through the centre of Vietnam visiting Ho Chi Min, Da Nang and Hoi An, staying in hotels along the way. They have visited the base camp in Nepal twice, once with a guide and then went with 15 members of their tramping club. The couple spent four weeks in Peru walking Machu Picchu, 7,000 feet above sea level in the Andean mountain range and have climbed Mount Kilimanjaro and Mount Kenya in Africa.

Paula and her friends on the summit on Mount Kenya

Undaunted, the couple are currently planning to walk the Pilgrim Trails in France. Looking ahead Paula intends to carry on doing the things she and her husband have always enjoyed doing, seizing opportunities as they arise, living a full and active lifestyle, whilst maintaining connection with family and the community.

TIM ORRELL

Tim, the eldest of two children was born in Lythan St. Annes in Blackpool England. Tragically, his father, and an uncle, were killed in a horrifying hit and run accident when Tim was only four years old. Tim's mother, who worked at Risley Remand Centre (now Risley Prison), raised her two children as a single parent in Culcheth, a large village near Warrington in Cheshire. Growing up, Tim wasn't sure what he wanted to do when he left school and was considering his options. A friend of the family had a brother in the Merchant Navy. The opportunity to see the world while he worked appealed to Tim, so he took the train to Liverpool and presented himself at the Peer Head Shipping Federation to find out more about the Merchant Navy. Following this meeting, Tim was offered a cadetship with the Merchant Navy and off he went to Fleetwood Nautical College in Lancashire to complete his pre-sea training programme.

When Tim graduated from Fleetwood Nautical College, he went to work for the Blue Star Line Shipping Company as a Deck Cadet. He was assigned to the 'Auckland Star', which sailed back and forth between the United Kingdom and New Zealand. Auckland was his first port of call and they would load New Zealand lamb, butter and wool, in ports around New Zealand.

Tim on deck

Tim enjoyed life at sea, and he appreciated his time onshore in both the United Kingdom and New Zealand. In 1979, he was working on the 'New Zealand Star's' maiden voyage, when the vessel experienced engine problems at sea.

The New Zealand Star's maiden voyage

It was quite stressful as Tim and his fiancée Yvonne, were getting married and he needed to get back to England in time for the wedding. In the end, he and two of his colleagues were flown home, and happily the big day went ahead as planned.

Tim and Yvonne's Wedding Day

Over time, whilst working for Blue Star Line, Tim progressed through the ranks from a Cadet to become Chief Officer and obtain his Master's Certificate.

Tim in his uniform showing his rank of Second Mate

In 1983, the Blue Star Line reduced the number of ships in its fleet and Tim, along with many others, was made redundant. By this time Tim and his wife had two young children and had just bought a house. It was a big blow, but luckily, he managed to get another job as First Mate on the supply boats servicing the Gas and Oil offshore industry in the North Sea. Working in the North Sea was not only hard work, it was dangerous, and the shifts were quite hard on the family as he was away from home for six-weeks and then home for six-weeks.

In 1986, Tim became the Assistant Operations Manager, responsible for the tug services in the port of Bristol and the whole family moved to the south west coast of England. He really enjoyed managing the port operations and the ships in the Bristol Channel and South Wales with 10 tugs and tug crew of 56. Tim remained in this role for the next 11 years. When ready for his next challenge he applied, trained and passed his exams to become a Marine Pilot. As a Marine Pilot he worked for Associated British Ports, the biggest port operation in the United Kingdom. Starting as a Class 3 Marine Pilot responsible for bringing in small ships, he worked his way up through the ranks to become a First-Class Marine Pilot, in Cardiff, Barry and Newport, with the responsibility for bringing in the big ships.

Meanwhile, as the children were growing up, Tim and Yvonne had been thinking about emigrating to either Australia or New Zealand. Several of Tim's marine colleagues had got jobs in New Zealand and Tim was familiar with the territory, but it wasn't the right time for the family. Coincidentally the connection with New Zealand was quite astonishing. One day, out of the blue, Tim's mother revealed that she had been married before she met and married Tim's father. Her first husband had been in the Royal Airforce and the couple had two children – a son called Richard and a daughter named Carol. This meant that Tim and his brother had a half-sister and a half-brother from their Mum's previous marriage they didn't know they had. Regrettably, her first husband had met someone else, and took off to New Zealand taking their children Richard and Carol with him. It was a heart- breaking situation. At the time Tim's mother had no idea where they had gone. In New

Zealand, the two children remembered their mother but couldn't contact her. Years later when the children grew up, Carol traced her mother through the Salvation Army. It's a remarkable experience to be reunited with your adult children after all these years, and incredible for Tim and his brother to learn they had siblings and to meet them for the first time when they had families of their own. To celebrate their 25th Wedding Anniversary Tim and Yvonne visited New Zealand and spent time with their new-found extended family in Tauranga.

In 2007, Tim was offered a job as a Marine Pilot in New Plymouth, New Zealand. Tim had turned 50 years of age when he and his wife Yvonne made the life-changing decision to emigrate. By this time both of their children were at University, both had partners and neither of them wanted to up-sticks and move to the other side of the world with their parents.   Tim and Yvonne courageously packed up their household possessions and shipped them out to New Zealand in a container and put their family home on the market.

In New Plymouth, things didn't quite work out as planned, so the couple moved to Wellington. In the capital city Yvonne got a dream job as a Nurse Educator in the private sector teaching people all over the lower part of the North Island how to use specialist equipment. Tim applied for a job on the Interislander Ferry – the Cook Strait three-hour ferry service that sails the 70 kilometres between Wellington in the North Island and Picton in the South Island. Initially Tim was offered a Third Mate role, a position he was overqualified for, but he took it anyway.   This was a 'Walk on Walk off' job on the 'Aratere', which meant that he did one trip from Wellington to Picton and back again – an eight-hour shift, and then he went home. The job was rostered six-days on and four-days off, with three rotating shifts - six consecutive early morning shifts, six afternoon shifts, and six-night shifts. Within two months, given his experience, Tim was promoted to Second Mate and his shift changed to seven days on (when he had to live in a cabin on board the ferry), and seven days off.

Once again Tim worked his way through the ranks, got promoted to First Mate and then completed his Master's Certificate to become a Captain.   The Cook Strait is considered one of the most dangerous and unpredictable waters in the world. The strait has an average depth of 128 metres, the topography is complex, and it is dominated by strong tidal flows. Rough water and heavy swells from strong winds are often experienced, especially from the south. The crossing requires strong purpose-built ferries and incredible skill to operate them safely. Tim was Captain of both the 'Arahura Ferry' – a 150 metre ship purpose built for the Cook Strait, and the 'Aratere Ferry' (180 metres in length). While Tim was employed with the Interislander, the Aratere Ferry was cut in half and extended by an additional 30 metres to carry more rail, vehicles and up to 500 passengers.

As Captain of these ferries it was Tim's responsibility to make difficult decisions under pressure to skilfully sail and dock these ships in all kinds of weather. Safety is paramount, but delays in sailing upsets everyone. It's a tough, but necessary call. As Captain, Tim worked 12-hour shifts docking and sailing six times per shift with his crew, in all kinds of conditions adhering to health and safety requirements within strict time constraints. The Aratere did three trips a day – a trip being three-hours 10 minutes each way, with only 50-minutes in dock to load and unload passengers, vehicles and cargo. Everything had to run like clockwork. It only needed one hiccup to blow the schedule. Tim worked for the Interislander for nine and a half years – four and a half of those as Master (Captain). Unfortunately, after the best part of a lifetime at sea, Tim unexpectedly experienced a dizzy spell on one of the ferry crossings. A second attack occurred shortly after and he sought medical help. Regrettably, he did not pass the medical and was forced to stand down from his position and take early retirement.

In the years since, Tim and Yvonne have relocated to the Kapiti Coast. Tim has part shares in a boat with two friends and frequently goes fishing with his pals. He regularly plays golf, is a committee member of a local community club, belongs to Rotary and volunteers at the Citizens Advice Bureau. Both of the couple's children are now married and they still live in England, so Tim and Yvonne have made several trips to see them. Now that Tim and Yvonne are semi-retired, they are able to stay in Europe for two to three months at a time visiting the family and take the opportunity vacation in different destinations either on their own or with friends. When they were in paid work, they could only take leave from their jobs for four to five weeks at time. Tim and Yvonne have joined 'Trusted House Sitters', an organisation that connects homeowners with reviewed and verified sitters who take care of their homes and pets while they are away. Tim says, "it's a great service for only a small annual fee" (approximately $130 per year at the time of writing). Tim and Yvonne have done a two-week house-sit themselves, and they have had house-sitters in their own home while they have been on holiday, which as Tim say, 'takes the worry out of leaving your own home for long periods of time.'

2019 was an incredibly special year for Tim and his family. Firstly, Tim celebrated his 65th birthday, and as such became eligible for his superannuation. Secondly, Tim and Yvonne celebrated their 40th Wedding Anniversary and were in Britain for the arrival of their daughter's first child, which was their second grandchild.   Tim has no plans to return to the United Kingdom to live, as travel is so much easier now. He is looking forward to a fulfilling retirement enjoying his hobbies with a close connection to the community in which he lives.

MIKE HARTLE

Mike, the first of four children, was born in Hayfield, Derbyshire in the United Kingdom. When he was ten years old his family emigrated to New Zealand where he and his three younger brothers initially went to primary school in Pukerua Bay. Shortly after arriving in New Zealand, Mike's parents bought a section in Paraparaumu Beach and his father, who was a skilled carpenter and cabinet maker, had a house built as a family home. At the time Paraparaumu Beach, a small beach community, was expanding. New houses and local amenities were being built as more and more families moved further up the coast from Wellington. When the family moved into their new home Mike became a foundation pupil at Paraparaumu Beach School and as a teenager attended Kapiti College.

Mike managed to obtain an apprenticeship as a Motor Mechanic at Paraparaumu Motor Engineers when he left school. It was here that Mike learned his trade in a large mechanical workshop. He also enjoyed arc and gas welding and had the opportunity to work on a wide variety of mechanical projects both on and off the job. As a young man he built several off-road buggies from Ford Popular cars with ten horsepower motors and with two gear boxes with his friends, and had great fun riding them in the bush in the Maungakotukutuku Valley. Later he also restored several motor bikes. As a mechanic he often worked 'the on-call' tow wagon, attending breakdowns and crashes and heavy truck retrieval in the Kapiti district. When he was rostered 'on-call' he had to stay local and contactable to be able to respond to those in need. In those days there were no mobile phones, but there was a phone at the local picture theatre, which at that time, was located on the corner of McLean Street and Kapiti Road at Paraparaumu Beach. Like many young people, Mike enjoyed going to the movies and this is where he met Dale, who was an usherette, who would let him know when he was required for the tow truck. This arrangement worked very well, and over time, the couple became good friends.

Mike was interested in all kinds of vehicles, and when he had completed his apprenticeship, it seemed a natural transition for him to join the Ministry of Transport as a Traffic Officer in 1975. His new role was stationed in Porirua and involved shift work, so he re-located from Paraparaumu to a small flat in Plimmerton to be closer to his work. Later the same year, Mike and Dale were married, and moved to a more suitable flat in Linden. While living in the flat, the couple worked hard to save for a home of their own. Eighteen months later, Mike took a job as a Security Officer at Wellington Airport. During this period the newly-weds purchased a section and spent their weekends building their family home in Whitby. It became clear that the rotating shift work and the commute into Wellington hindered the speed of their building project, so Mike took a job at Linden Motors, a local garage which was much closer to home, and went back to his trade as a motor mechanic. Eventually all the hard work paid off and the couple moved into their own home in 1978.

In 1980, the family expanded with the arrival of their first twin boys, followed nine years later by a second set of twin boys. Mike recalls being very involved in the children's activities while they were growing up, for example, when his children were in the cubs and scouts, Mike was a Scout

Leader. He remembers a very proud moment when his older twins were presented with their Queens Scout Awards by the Governor General at Government House in Wellington. Mike had also received the Queen Scout Award many years before. Throughout these years Mike also pursued his own hobbies, involving the family as much as possible. He built his own off roader in his garage when the first set of twins were toddlers and was always interested in trains. His Dad had bought him a Hornby Dublo train layout when he was a child, which had aroused his lifelong interest in both model and full-sized trains.

While the children were growing up, the family went on many camping holidays together. One year, while they were holidaying at the Arataki Motor Camp in Havelock North, Mike and Dale were looking for things to do with the boys, when they spotted a brochure for 'Keirunga Park Railway'. They thought they would give it a go and took the children to the park for a ride on the various trains including steam trains.

Mike's brother Peter is at the rear, his son Zane is at the front. Mike and Dale's four boys, Jason, Aaron, Blair and Callum are in the middle.

The whole family really enjoyed the experience as captured in the photo taken at Keirunga Park Railway. While they were there, Mike talked to some of the drivers who were running the trains and found out that they had built the locomotives and the track at the park. He was so inspired he made the decision then and there to build his own locomotive and passenger carriage. Influenced by what these guys had achieved, Mike came back from the family holiday and shared his experience with some friends. He joined a model Railway club at Marine Gardens in Raumati, (Kapiti Live Steamers). Later he joined the 'Hutt Valley Model Engineers' at Petone, and in 2002, the 'Havelock North Live Steamers', and so began his new hobby. He researched the design for his locomotive, a diesel based on original designs, and deliberately planned and built it slightly over scale to accommodate a car engine.

Mike knew that building the locomotive would be an expensive and long-term project and recognised his family responsibilities were his first priority. Nevertheless, he was motivated to complete his first locomotive engine, the DG760, for the 10th Anniversary of 'Havelock North Live Steamers' held in Havelock North, Easter 2002. Following simple drawings, he used his mechanical skills and experience to make most of the parts for his locomotive using hand and portable power tools. The wheels, axles and bogie side frames he had specially made by Harold, who was a member of the 'Hutt Valley Model Engineers'. He proudly christened his finished and painted locomotive 'The Mistress', a name that Dale came up with, at the Easter opening weekend at Havelock North. All of the family attended this event.

Mike driving his DG760

This was only the beginning of what was to become a life-long passion. Dale became interested too, often joining Mike at train events. This was a great opportunity for her to relax and even drive the trains as well as she had passed her licence to drive them at Havelock North, which is recognised as a challenging track.

Dale driving the "Mistress" at Kapiti Miniature Railway at Raumati Beach.

Six years later, at the 2008 International Live Steam Convention in Manukau Auckland, Mike won the 'Best Diesel Locomotive' award for his locomotive, which Mike and his family regard as a great honour. He subsequently built three ride-on articulated passenger carriages for the 2010 Convention at Nelson, with padded seats and footrails, all painted the same colour as the locomotive, so they are a matching set. He made a purpose-built trailer to transport the locomotive and carriages, which incidentally weighs nearly half a ton. His DG760 locomotive has run on several public and private tracks in the North and South Islands.

Grandson Astin,
learning to drive the County Donegal Rail Bus at Petone

Mike has since made and purchased several additional trains, including two small electric (battery powered) railbuses that can be driven by children under supervision, an EC09 battery electric locomotive, and a caboose carriage for which he has built a chassis to put the carriage on.

Over the years, Mike's working life continued to revolve around transport. When driver licence testing was privatised in New Zealand, he became a Driver Licence Testing Officer in April 1998. Ten years later, he re-trained as a Driving Instructor and for the next 11 years he operated his own independent driving school, during which time he also facilitated Defensive Driving courses in the community.

Dale with granddaughter Sophie on the EC09

The EC09

Prior to retiring, Mike and Dale attended a couple of retirement seminars. By this time, their children had grown up, and they now have four grandchildren, two of whom live in Australia. The couple had always planned to relocate further north, and not long after Mike retired aged 65, the couple moved to Levin in the Horowhenua. Thinking about the longer term they bought a single-story home, with no stairs, on a flat section. Mike now has a much bigger garage to accommodate his trains and the train trailers, and still has plenty of room for his other projects. Fortuitously, within weeks of moving into their new home, Dale picked up a tutoring role at the Horowhenua Learning Centre, so the couple began to become part of the fabric of their new community.

Since moving to Levin, Mike has built two new mobile work benches for his workshop, five train carriages - one for himself and four for his club, plus six refurbished carriages, and is currently in the process of building a petrol tanker carriage. He has built and accumulated quite a bit of track and has set up a working railway track with his friend in Levin. The track is being built primarily for their own enjoyment, but they may open it to visiting railway friends from time to time in the future. Mike's hobby has been enduring throughout most of his adult life. It has been an opportunity to meet, learn and share with like-minded people and their families both in New Zealand and overseas. He is able to utilise his creativity, skills and experience, achieve a sense of accomplishment and fulfilment, and bring so much joy to his own family and the wider community.

Looking ahead, Mike and Dale have made significant lifestyle changes, while at the same time maintaining their hobbies. The couple are planning a big family celebration when Dale retires and intend to take an extended trip to the United Kingdom next year. They also plan to spend plenty of time having fun with their grandchildren

For more information about Mike's locomotives and park railways in New Zealand check out his website http://www.webgirl.co.nz/dg760/

GRAEME

Graeme, a scientist, worked in the Horticultural Research Centre at Levin, before becoming a Research Fellow at Victoria University. The research project he was working on was externally funded and although it was envisaged that the contract for the research would be renewed, this was not the case. Graeme was only 61 years of age and had no plans to retire. Money was not an issue, but Graeme had so much to contribute and had to re-think his future.

At that time Graeme and his partner enjoyed grinding their own coffee beans, experimented making coffee and socialised with others who also enjoyed a chat over a cuppa. One day, he shared his interest in making coffee, when he was purchasing his beans from his supplier. By chance, the supplier offered Graeme a place on a Barista course where he would be trained and certificated.   This chance opportunity was to be the catalyst that expanded his interest in coffee and changed the direction of Graeme's career.

Within a short period of time Graeme had made the decision to set up a coffee cart in Levin and start his own business. He diligently researched the feasibility of his idea, looked at several different coffee carts and came across a person who could build a coffee cart from scratch. He developed the relationship with the builder and together they designed and built the coffee cart. Meanwhile Graeme investigated an appropriate location for his business and settled on a site on the main road where he would be in a good position to attract local and passing traffic.   He researched and completed all the necessary business details, got certificated with the local council, purchased his coffee and gained approval to open for business in January 2013. When Graeme checked his records, he noted that he had sold 19 cups of coffee on his first day and averaged 15 cups of coffee per day over the first week he was in business. Since then his business has grown exponentially.

At the time of writing Graeme has been in business for more than six years. He is very customer focused and relationship orientated – folk matter, and therefore he serves good coffee and operates his business around the needs of the people. His customers want coffee early in the morning from 6.45am, so that's when he starts work and will stay open for as long as his customers are there both for a coffee and social connection. Graeme develops a relationship with people explaining that they come to see him at the coffee cart, it's a social activity, especially for his regulars who have become good friends. As he says "If they like the coffee and know you'll be there for them, they return. It's a customer building process". Graeme doesn't see his business as work. Recognising he is providing a service and reliability counts, he opens seven days a week to service his customers, including Christmas Day.

Over the years Graeme has become very knowledgeable about coffee and has developed a strong relationship with his supplier, Flight Coffee, to the extent that he was given the opportunity to visit Columbia and Rwanda to experience first-hand at grass-roots level how coffee is grown and processed. Graeme was particularly keen to support projects working with local Columbian farmer co-operatives to receive an ethical price for growing and processing their coffee. This model resonated with Graeme, with the aim to assist development of the local people, rather than multinational coffee companies making huge profits while depriving the growers of a living wage. The visits to coffee origins were great learning experiences as he was exposed to the whole process – growing, milling, sorting and drying.

Graeme doesn't consider himself to be an expert, as he said he is a scientist. He likes to learn new things and appreciated the opportunity to talk with the growers, get to know them and find out how they had adapted and changed over the years. He learned that as the farmers became more educated about producing high quality beans, they picked only the ripe coffee cherries thus raising the quality of their coffee. At the same time, they moved from piecework pay (financial reward based on volume, regardless of whether the cherries were ripe or not) to a salary, a concept that was initially a challenge for the farmers to grasp. Graeme said his three weeks in Columbia was "an eye opener". He developed an affinity with the people, gave him a sense of his place in the process and his contribution to this community, and could share this story with his customers back in New Zealand.

Graeme has since been to Rwanda at the invitation of his coffee supplier where he met and worked alongside the people who work as a community to produce their coffee. Graeme recalls the absolute joy the people showed when they welcomed buyers onto their workstations. Knowing the whole process in action, meeting and developing a relationship with the people and knowing he is part of the end-to-end ethical process is very motivating for Graeme, who now purchases Rwandan coffee from a small nation producing great coffee.

Graeme is doing things differently. He generates his own income through his business, which for him, is a lifestyle. He provides a consumer and social service for his own community, is part of an international process that is totally ethical, supporting a community 14,000 kilometres away on the other side of the world, and shares this story with his customers who can appreciate that they too are part of this process.

Graeme is now taking things to the next level experimenting in coffee competitions for the right to represent New Zealand in international coffee competitions. His first competition was for the Brewers Cup in 2016. Encouraged he has since entered the Aeropress Competition making filter coffee. He is recognised as the oldest competitor world-wide. On reflection Graeme said he never knew that this was his destiny, for him it's all about purpose, passion, people and the energy to follow through. Graeme has no plans to retire – he's a spiritual person providing a meaningful, connected community service.

MARIE HANNAN

Marie was born in Bluff, the southernmost town in mainland New Zealand. She is the seventh of ten children, and the youngest of the five daughters in the family. Her Grandmother lived on Stewart Island (Rakiura). This is a small community comprising a few hundred people, just 30 kilometres south of the South Island across the Foveaux Strait, which is a rough and often treacherous stretch of water. Her parents also came from large families within this close-knit community. Marie's father Lewis Alfred Dawson, colloquially known as 'Boun', was a fisherman. He was very well known and respected, and her parent's whanau were very close. Sadly, immense tragedy struck this family when two of Marie's older sisters drowned. When Marie was only two years old her father was killed in a road accident. As can be expected, the family and the wider community were grief stricken.

During these tough times, Marie's mother needed practical assistance to help raise the family so Marie and her older sister Liz, went to live with their Auntie Naomi and Uncle 'Hup' in Port Chalmers in Dunedin, 240 kilometres away from home. Marie and Liz loved living with Naomi and Hup, who had no children of their own. It was a loving family where Marie looked to her Auntie as her mother during the five years that they lived together. Marie recalls how on Friday nights, she and Liz entertained their Aunt and Uncle and her Auntie Naomi's sisters, telling stories, reciting poems and singing songs for them. Marie's mother visited whenever she could, and the girls were re-united with their siblings in Invercargill when her mother re-married.

Marie went to school in Invercargill and met June, one of her life-long friends at Rosedale Intermediate School. She remembers spending the school holidays on Stewart Island with her Grandmother with whom she was very close. Growing up she enjoyed swimming at the beach and learned lots of crafts. When Marie left school, she worked in a local Accountants office for a year. Her friend June was training to be a Community Nurse in Invercargill, and as she was enjoying it so much, she persuaded Marie to join her. Marie also trained as a Community Nurse (now known as an Enrolled Nurse) and, once registered, chose to work on the surgical ward at Kew Hospital in Invercargill, which she loved.

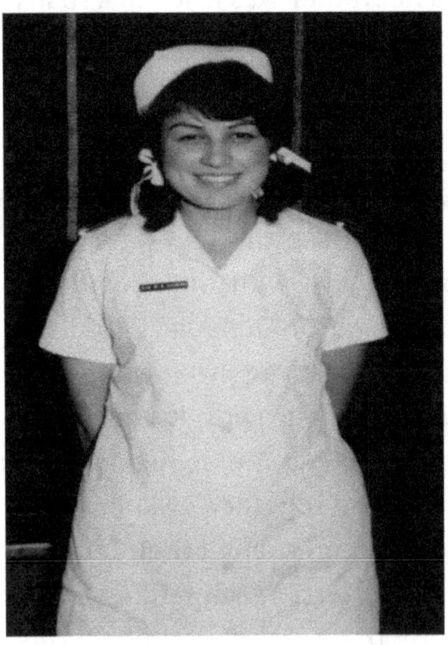

Marie Hannan

As a nurse Marie learned a lot about people and more about her own family. When patients and staff found out who she was, people began giving her crayfish and mutton birds etc. as gifts because they remembered her Dad and her grandparents, liked them, and regarded them as highly respected members of the community. These gestures made Marie realise that her family were very special people. Learning more about them from others was like having a family reunion. While nursing at Kew, Marie's Grandmother broke her hip and was admitted as a patient, so Marie regularly spent time with her while she recuperated. Reflecting on these days Marie said 'I'm proud to be related to my Grandmother. She was such a caring person who loved people'.

While working at Kew, Marie met Neville whom she later married. Neville worked in the laboratory at the local Milk Treatment Centre, and later shifted to the Tisbury Cheese Factory. Neville wanted to become a cheesemaker so for three months each year for three years he attended Massey University to complete his training. While studying at Massey, he was offered a job as a cheesemaker at New Zealand (NZ) Rennet Co., in Taranaki. Although the couple had just bought their first home, the opportunity was too good to miss, so they rented out their family home and moved to Eltham. Neville loved his new role and was very highly regarded, and Marie went nursing at Hawera Hospital. The couple settled into the local community and became close friends with Ross and Glenys McCallum from Hawera. In due course, both of Marie and Neville's children were born in Taranaki and the couple built their home here.

Over time Neville became an expert cheesemaker and was widely recognised as being progressive and successful in his field. Ross who was an entrepreneur, was keen to partner with Neville who was the expert cheese maker to set up their own specialised cheese factory. Marie, Neville, Glenys and Ross formed a partnership and moved their families to the Kapiti Coast where they set up their new venture 'Kapiti Cheeses'. Marie and Neville sold their family home in Taranaki and worked hard to raise their share of the capital to establish the purpose-built cheese factory at Lindale. Neville project-managed the building of the factory and designed the stainless-steel moulds so that the cheese could be made in the old-fashioned way. Marie found a house to live in, went nursing three days a week, sold Avon products from home to help raise the capital for the business, and looked after the children. Marie also custom made the cheesecloth covers, in various sizes, for the cheese to go into the custom-made moulds.

It took two years to get the cheese factory up and running. Neville initially specialised in Gouda and Cheddar cheese, the former taking three months to make, and the latter taking up to one year to make before it is ready to sell as 'Tasty Cheese' to the public. Marie became the Company Secretary for the business managing the accounts and the administration. Ross and Neville organised an all-year-round supply of milk and the cheese factory operated seven days a week. The two couples worked very hard and took turns to work on the weekends. It was a huge success story. Within two years of opening the factory, Kapiti Cheeses had won prestigious awards. The New Zealand Dairy Board offered Neville a consultancy role which involved extensive travel overseas and eventually he was offered a three-year contract in California. Neville trained David Orchard as a Cheesemaker as well as Ross to enable the business to continue to run in his absence. The price was to give up the day-to-day management of Kapiti Cheeses, but it was a great opportunity and Marie and the family were keen to give it a go, so the family moved to Santa Rosa, California.

Sadly, things didn't work out for the family in California and Neville and Marie parted ways. Marie returned to New Zealand with the children and set up her own home on the Kapiti Coast. For the next six years she took on cleaning jobs to supplement the family's income and later worked as a nurse at Paraparaumu Hospital until it closed in 1995. When the new retirement villages opened, she took on two part-time nursing roles, working the night duty rosters as this was close to home. When the family grew up, Marie looked for a new challenge. She re-trained as a Real Estate Agent and for the next nine years she thoroughly enjoyed this job. During this period, she made several trips to India to undertake outreach work through her church.

Marie in India

Meanwhile Kapiti Cheeses continued to thrive. By this time, the business had 144 shareholders, the majority of which were held by Neville, Marie, Ross and Glenys. A buyer approached the company, and 75% of the shareholders voted to sell their shares, so the business was sold. Marie invested her share in the property market, went on holidays and visited family overseas, but found she felt guilty about the money and questioned her lifestyle. She spent some time reflecting on what was important. She said she wanted to do something purposeful – something she really enjoyed. Marie, at 53 years of age, made a life-changing courageous decision to move to Nepal to work as a volunteer teacher for two years. Just like that, Marie packed a few belongings and travelled 12,000 kilometres to Damak in the province of Jhapa, Nepal, which is approximately two hours from the Indian border. She had never been there before and didn't know anyone in the 30,000 community. The job came with free accommodation, and she lived off her savings. On arrival Marie got involved with the Christian community, dressed and lived like the locals, either walked or used local transport, and volunteered to help wherever she could. In Nepal there was very high unemployment (48%) and most of the men went to the big cities to get work. To put this into perspective, Damak is approximately 12-14 hours by road on a good day, with no strikes, to get to Kathmandu – it can take up to 25 hours to travel this distance, and it wasn't always safe to make this trip.

Regardless, Marie loved the Nepalese. She became so engaged with the community that she remained in Damak as a volunteer at her own expense for four years. During this time, several non-government organisations (NGO's) came to Nepal to teach the women how to make things with the intention of being able to create a sustainable income. The women learned how to knit, felt, make jewellery etc., but tourists do not visit the villages, so the villagers wouldn't be able to sell what they produced. Marie identified an opportunity. When she returned home, she could help the Nepalese by purchasing their goods, thus creating employment opportunities for the villagers, and selling them in New Zealand.

Back in New Zealand, energised with her ideas, Marie who was then aged 57, started a business called 'Nepal-New Zealand Connection'. She purchased her goods directly from a Nepalese woman living in Nepal, air freighted the goods to New Zealand, and stored them in her garage and in her station wagon. Marie bought some folding tables and became a regular stall holder at markets in Otaki, Foxton, Sanson, Paraparaumu and Wellington. Open for business, people flocked to purchase her unique merchandise, especially the garments made from natural fibres such as hemp, cotton and wool - for example hats, gloves and jackets, which are made by the Nepalese with New Zealand wool. Through word of mouth, regulars flocked to her stalls and her business boomed.

Marie yearned to open a shop so she could have a more permanent site for her business. When she turned 65, she cashed in her Kiwisaver superannuation savings and trialled this idea for three months in Te Horo and became part of a cooperative community in Shannon. Learning from the experience she took the plunge and opened a small shop on the main highway in Paraparaumu, which was so successful she needed to move to bigger premises. Now the 'Nepal-New Zealand Connection' is located on Coastlands Parade. Marie is very clear on the purpose of her business and manages it on her own terms. Her shop is open Tuesday-Saturday, 10am-5pm and she employs people who have an affinity with the Nepalese and the products they create. She really enjoys her life and her work and knows she is making a difference. In her words "it's a treasure trove and is getting Nepal known". Marie continues to operate 'pop-up' stalls at the Martinborough Fair, World of Wearable Art, Waipukurau and Otaki markets, as she has developed a relationship with her regulars in these locations.

Marie's shop in Paraparaumu

In 2019, the Hillary Commission, (now known as Sport and Recreation New Zealand – SPARC), celebrated what would have been Sir Edmund Hillary's 100th birthday. Apart from his achievements, Sir Edmund Hillary was renowned for his affinity with the Nepalese. As part of the celebrations representatives from the Hillary Commission visited Marie in her shop, talked to her about her life in Nepal, and learned more about her goal – the 'Nepal-New Zealand Connection'. It was a great honour. Marie was thrilled that they sought her out and purchased goods themselves. The representatives were inspired by what a single person can achieve when they put their mind to it.

Marie life journey is an incredible story. Clearly, she shows us that age is no barrier to helping others while at the same time leading a purposeful, productive and fulfilling life.

If you'd like to know more about the Nepal-NZ Connection check it out on Facebook Nepal-NZ-Connection or contact Marie at nigsmum3a@gmail.com

COLIN DICKEY

Colin grew up in Lower Hutt. When he was 15 years of age, he left school and went to work for Hannah's shoe shop in Lambton Quay, Wellington. He really enjoyed his job with this retail chain store, and within 12 months he was sent on a management course. To get more experience he was later transferred to Hannah's store in Petone that serviced a niche market. While he enjoyed retail, as a young man he was interested in fashion, and he missed working in the city with exposure to a broad range of clientele. By the time Colin was 17, he changed jobs transitioning from shoes to menswear and was working in the much bigger retail area in Lower Hutt. He loved the nature of this work and was good at it, so within a short space of time he became quite well known in the trade and was head-hunted by other menswear stores.

Reflecting back Colin recalls the life changing moment when he met a successful businessman named Bill Sinnett at a Christmas party. Bill owned the Sinnett Menswear store in NaeNae and another store in the Wainuiomata Mall. Shortly after Colin joined his company, Bill purchased the menswear business previously owned by the Hutt Valley Co-op. This store saw the birth of a new name and became known as Centre Menswear. Bill not only offered Colin a job, he took him under his wing and became a mentor and second father to him. Bill taught his protégé everything he knew about retail and took Colin to the warehouses when he was purchasing stock. Over the years the mentor/mentee relationship blossomed, and the menswear stores were very successful. It was a massive blow when Bill died suddenly in

1977. In 1978, Colin and his wife Kathy were approached by Bill's two silent business partners to manage the menswear shops with a 10% shareholding. Colin accepted the offer. He gradually bought the other two partners out and expanded his business from there. When the landlord sold the NaeNae building the owner required the site. Colin decided it was time to move on from NaeNae and opened a new shop in Lower known as Centre Menswear. Shortly after this the Wainuiomata store was sold to Warnocks.

While living in Lower Hutt, Colin and Kathy had three children. One summer, the family had a fabulous beach holiday on the Kapiti Coast. Colin had lived in Lower Hutt for 29 years, but the family holiday became the catalyst for change. Colin and Kathy sold their family home in the Hutt Valley, bought a house in Raumati South and the family moved to the Kapiti Coast where the children went to school. Colin commuted to his businesses in Lower Hutt, then made the decision to open a store in the Coastlands Mall and another in the K Mart Plaza in Porirua. He also opened a surf/streetwear store in Coastlands called 'Havoc'. Kathy, who also worked in retail had her own womenswear store in Coastlands called 'Tactix', which she owned and managed for 14 years. Moreover, Colin, with a partner in Auckland began to import and distribute clothing to major stores in New Zealand including James Smiths, Ballantynes, and Kirkcaldie and Stains. The businesses flourished and the couple were very successful business owner/operators for more than 30 years.

Regrettably, as the decades passed, everything changed in the retail trade. Rapid technological change, access to online shopping from around the world via the internet, and the global financial crisis had an enormous impact on the New Zealand economy as it did overseas. Independent retail stores throughout the country were hit hard. As the leases for his stores came up for renewal, Colin looked long and hard at the balance sheets and realised business wasn't growing. After 30 years Colin made the decision to close his stores. The last two shops Colin and Kathy closed were Tactix and Centre Menswear located in Coastlands Shopping Centre.

Colin and Kathy had planned to retire when they closed their retail businesses. Colin still owned his importing company, and, in this capacity, he travelled overseas for a couple of months at a time to buy merchandise. In his spare time, he played golf - but Colin and Kathy had always worked, and realised they wanted more. In Colin's words 'we wanted to reinvent ourselves'. Around this time Colin had a major back operation, and, as part of his rehabilitation programme with the Accident Compensation Corporation, he went on a course to get his passenger (P) endorsement – a licence to carry passengers for hire or reward, with the intention of looking for a part-time job. Reflecting on his skills and experience Colin knew he liked driving, really enjoyed working with people, was very customer focused, liked his independence and needed purposeful activity to get him out of the house. As luck would have it, on completion of the course, he saw an advertisement in the local paper for a part-time shuttle driver. He applied for and got the job and started work the next day. He really liked the role and the flexibility this type of work offered. Unfortunately, while on holiday in Australia, the business owner made the decision to close the business and subsequently held a farewell lunch for all the part-time drivers. It was disappointing as the shuttle service was highly valued by the clients that used it.

Time elapsed while Colin and Kathy re-considered their options. They missed the challenge of owning and operating a business and came up with the idea of running their own shuttle service. They began to research how to run this type of enterprise, for example setting up a booking system for a seven-day week, 24 hours a day service, with vehicles etc., which was different from the retail trade. They liaised with the owner of the previous shuttle company that had closed down, and subsequently purchased the phone number and two of the vehicles that were no longer being used. Colin, who was 65 years old at the time, and Kathy registered their new business 'Kapiti Coast Shuttles' with New Zealand's Companies Office and put a full-page advertisement in the Kapiti Observer marketing the service. Kathy managed the bookings and two of the drivers who had previously worked with Colin came to work for him, and between them they provided a service to the community.

At the time of writing, Kapiti Coast Shuttles has been operating for more than five years. It's a thriving business - they now employ eight part-time drivers all of whom are semi-retired. One of the two drivers who initially joined the company is still working for the service, while the other driver recently left to return to the New Zealand Symphony Orchestra. The business is expanding all the time and does not compete with the local taxi service. Most of the jobs (80%) are 'pick up and drop offs' to/from Wellington Airport/Kapiti Coast. The remainder of the work is for corporate clients and round-trip hospital appointments providing a personal door to door service for those in need. Colin, Kathy and the team offer "a personal, friendly and reliable shuttle service to the community". They are always there ready and waiting for their clients when they arrive at the airport, no matter how long delays may be.

This is not only a success story, it's a way of life and a fulfilling pursuit for Colin and Kathy in semi-retirement. It's a testament that we can learn new skills, gain a qualification, research and successfully set-up a new business, provide an exceptional and appreciated service for the community, and create jobs for others in later life. As Colin and Kathy run their semi-retirement business from home, they can, and do, spend plenty of time with their three children and seven grandchildren who live in the district. They also enjoy pursuing their own interests and hobbies.

In 2019, Colin and Kathy celebrated their 70th birthdays with their whole family who joined them for a holiday in Noosa, Australia. It's never too late to pursue our passions, seek new opportunities, make big decisions, try new experiences, invest in our relationships, enjoy a good laugh and look forward to the future.

Colin and Kathy Dickey

For more information about Kapiti Coast Shuttles, check out this website www.kapiticoastshuttles.co.nz

CAROL MAHONEY

Carol worked in Information Technology for most of her working life. While it's mainly a male dominated profession, she had the opportunity to work on multiple projects, provide technical support, develop software and manage information systems for several organisations in New Zealand, London (where she lived for four years) and Canberra. After retiring from her substantive role as Chief Technical Officer for an Auckland firm, Carol and her husband thought long and hard about what they wanted to do and how they would spend their time.

They planned a trip to explore the Australian outback. They designed their own fully self-contained motorhome in Auckland and shipped it to Queensland Australia. They spent ten adventurous months travelling across the Northern Territory and all around the outer edges of this vast country. Carol then looked for a useful hobby and took up patchwork quilting. Carol discovered she enjoyed this artistic craft, became really good at it, and made each of her grandchildren two or three beautiful quilts. Encouraged by the feedback she received, Carol started a home-based online quilting business selling a range of quilting tools and accessories to others who were passionate about this hobby. In her early 60's she learned how to set up and run an online business from scratch, and attended quilting and craft shows all over the country and in Australia to sell her products.

Unfortunately, Carol's son Shaun had some major surgery which changed his career path significantly. Carol and Shaun explored the possibilities for the future, reflected on their combined skill sets and decided to start a new home-based online business developing online newsletters for small businesses. Carol drew on her expertise to develop the software and Shaun managed the sales and marketing. It was their first foray into business together, operating on both sides of the Tasman – Shaun in Australia and Carol in New Zealand. The partnership worked well, and the business was successful, but nearly three years later they realised that they weren't really enjoying it.

Shaun and Carol have cheerful, lively personalities and are very people centred. Talking it over they decided they wanted to have fun with their time and bring people together, rather than meet people at a distance through online newsletters. They toyed with some ideas and launched 'Sticky Handshake' – a small business network that connected people with one another. They established quite a few members and many discussions regarding the issue of loneliness, the biggest epidemic amongst the 55+ population, was raised. It became clear that when people leave work, they lose contact with one another. Although some people have lots of friends on Facebook, older people don't necessarily have the 'real life' personal connection they had when they were working and somewhere to go to meet people.

Carol and Shaun already knew they had the ability to run a business, what they wanted was to be passionate their work, while at the same provide a meaningful, worthwhile service for others. The idea of expanding the network both in New Zealand and in Australia, connecting people with new friends encouraging and enabling people to get out of the house to have fun together, appealed to them. They already had the software for this business in place, they just needed to change direction, tweak their business model and broaden their Network membership to people 55+. Initially they called their new business 'Chirpy Oldies', but quickly changed the name to 'Chirpy Plus'. To test the viability of their product they invited foundation members of the network to join for free. The response was amazing. The business clearly met a need in the community on both sides of the Tasman, and for some people it was a lifeline.

Now, 12 months on, Chirpy Plus operates a total subscription model. For a membership fee of only $8 a month – the price of two cups of coffee, 'Chirpies' can join any 'Catch Up' group where members meet in cafes for friendship and companionship. The network that brings people together face-to-face to meet new people and have fun together has rapidly expanded all over Australia and New Zealand. Hundreds of Chirpy group Catch Up meetings are taking place, each with a volunteer host who welcomes everyone, introduces people to one another, and helps facilitate the catch-up network meeting. These volunteers recognise that it's a big step for some people to join a group, but in no time, they make friends and enjoy a good laugh with others. Several of the Chirpy Catch Up groups have established Chirpy outings, walking groups and some even go on holiday together (check out the Chirpy Plus cruises) – activities people had not contemplated doing in the past. Popular forums including arts, crafts and other hobbies have been initiated amongst the members and people can play online bingo with Chirpy members all over Australia.

Carol Mahoney

Chirpy Plus is Carol's third start-up business since she 'retired' from her job as a Chief Technical Officer. Reflecting on the success of their social enterprise business, Carol, who is now 70 years young, appreciates you 'have to get it right when you start a business later in life, as you can't recover if things go wrong as easily as you can when you are much younger'. She says 'it's critical to do things you are passionate about that add value to others, then it doesn't seem like work at all' – it's a lifestyle. Carol says they 'only choose to work with nice people', and every week she and Shaun get to as many of the meetings as they can to establish personal contact with their members.

At the time of writing Chirpy Plus has a membership of 23,000 in Australasia. To ensure people stay connected over the Christmas New Year holiday, Chirpy Christmas picnics are arranged for their members. Carol and Shaun recognise this is a time when people who live alone feel most vulnerable and have proactively done something to ensure this does not happen for their members.

The service this business provides brings so much joy to thousands of people, including Carol and Shaun. Chirpy Plus now has investors who believe in the vision behind Chirpy Plus, which means that Chirpy Plus can grow outside Australasia. Carol and Shaun have built a business with a focus on families and have no intention of setting up corporate offices for either themselves or their staff of 18 people. Their staff love the idea that they do not need to commute to work and can build their working days around child minding or child school pickup timetables. Carol still manages the technology and Shaun manages the sales and marketing aspects of the business. The great news is that further expansion is on the horizon as this mother and son duo is planning to establish a Chirpy Plus network in the United States and the United Kingdom. Fired up with enthusiasm, retirement in the traditional sense is not an option for Carol – she is living life to the max!

Carol loves talking to younger people, encouraging them to look at tech as a career, especially girls. Carol is also proud of what she is achieving at her age and likes being a role model to prove that age is no barrier to what you can do.

Carol Mahoney

To learn more about Chirpy Plus check out these websites
www.ChirpyPlus.co.nz and www.ChirpyPlus.com.au

DAVID

David retired from the New Zealand Airforce following 25 years of service as an Engineering Officer. During his military service he worked both in New Zealand and overseas and reached the senior ranks. On retirement, he was still a relatively young man, so he looked forward to another career in 'civvy street'. He entered the corporate world with Databank where he initially worked as an Engineering Manager. Later, when Databank merged with another organisation to become Government Computer Services (GCS), he took on the challenging Human Resources Director role. David says he had always been a practical man and reflecting on his military service and his 10 years in the corporate scene he realised that although his work with Databank was practical in nature, it was very process orientated and he wasn't doing what he wanted to do. At this time in his life he wanted to be more creative and to be free to do what he wanted to do. He wanted to be his own boss and to live life on his own terms. Before leaving the corporate life, David embarked on a four-year course and attained a Diploma in Homeopathy from the Wellington College of Homeopathy. He became a Registered Homeopath and practised part time for about 10 years.

At 50 years of age, David radically changed his lifestyle. He purchased a family home on 55 acres of land with 150 sheep and made the decision to give up his day job to become a farmer. He had no previous farming experience but was very keen to learn. David said he planned everything. He had lots of ideas on what to do with his time and the land, knew exactly where he was going and immediately set to work developing the property. The house was in a bare paddock, so he developed a garden, planted hundreds of trees, installed a reliable water supply system and solar panels. As the farm is in a rural location, he installed traffic lights at the entrance to the long winding driveway and designed and built a computer-based alarm system with several sensors programmed to pick up visitors entering and leaving the farm. After a couple of years David realised that sheep farming wasn't for him, so he traded the sheep in and invested in highland cattle.

A couple of years later David considered others might also enjoy time out in the country, so he designed and built a retreat for small groups of people. This seven-bed accommodation is completely self-contained and over the last 20 years has been used by several families and organisations including church groups, women's and natural health groups. Next to the retreat is a large workshop that David uses to develop his projects.

A few years later David designed and built a large music and art studio for his wife Joy. The studio is modelled on a small church and is about the same size. Here Joy has her own space where she paints and plays the piano accordion.

The music and art studio

David and Joy's next project was to design and build a large gazebo in a scenic spot next to a pond complete with a waterwheel and ducks. David, Joy and their children and grandchildren and the guests staying at the retreat use the gazebo for barbeques and morning teas.

Along the journey, David got to know his neighbours, one of whom asked him to come and work for him for three months in their IT department. By this time David was in his late 50's, and as it was a fixed-term contract, he agreed to help his neighbour out. Time passed and the three-month contract kept getting extended, thus limiting the time David could pursue his own projects and manage his farm. As he was enjoying the work, he negotiated a part-time 20 hour per week contract, comprising two 10-hour days (Monday and Tuesdays), with overnight accommodation at the Nurses hostel enabling him to reduce the time spent commuting 60 kms each way each day to get to and from work. It was a win/win situation for everyone at the time and David continued to work in this role until he turned 60 years of age when he resigned in order to pursue his own interests.

In addition to farming, building and engineering projects David joined the Taoist Tai Chi Society which taught a gentle series of focused movements shown to have a positive effect on muscle strength, flexibility, balance and general wellbeing. Impressed with the results David trained to be a registered Tai Chi instructor and facilitates a weekly class to enable others to benefit from this practice. David loves music and became an accomplished ballroom and sequence dancer. For the past 20 years David has attended sequence dances once or twice a week and runs a Sunday afternoon Tea Dance each season. He organises the dance programme and researches and selects the best music possible for each dance, to ensure everyone who participates has an enjoyable experience. For both his 60th and 70th birthdays he and Joy hosted a dance, organised the music and provided a large hall to celebrate these memorable occasions with their family and friends. In his spare time David is writing a futuristic book, set in the 2020's with the working title 'The End of the Road'. The book is a work in progress aimed at challenging culturally accepted ways of thinking and raising awareness of many conspiracies adversely affecting the lives of people.

David's inspiration for his current project was instigated nearly 40 years ago when he was in the Airforce stationed in Washington DC. He recalls cycling near the Potomac River and hearing fabulous music coming from a fairground organ which was playing as the carousel was operating. He describes how he heard the 'happiest music on earth' and knew then and there that one day he would build one of his own. As with all of his projects David researched what he needed to do, using both the internet and books. Carefully thinking it through, he made a prototype building 30 pipes to test his ideas and was delighted with the sound they produced without speakers. He then specifically designed a fairground organ that would fit on a trailer to enable it to be easily transported from place to place. So far David has spent more than two years on this challenging project. It took him two months to build the first 30 pipes and during the last year he has since built six melody sets of pipes, in addition to two reed, two bass and three accompaniment sets. This is a lot of pipes and by the time he has finished the band organ will have over 300 pipes in total. He is looking forward to arranging some of the fairground organ's music himself.

David's band organ project

David ordered a large monkey puppet for the organ from the USA and with some adaptations, it will sit on the front of the organ and be able to speak to the people who come along to watch it. His overall aim is to entertain people at market days and fairs so that everyone can enjoy the atmosphere and the experience as our predecessors did.

David rises at about 6am most mornings and is on-the-go until around 7pm at night. He said he doesn't have the time or the inclination to blob out.   He makes time for the extended families, enjoys working on his projects, and there is always plenty to do on the property. He really enjoys living on the land, being part of nature, and appreciates the constantly changing landscape.

Reflecting on his life, David wonders if his life would have been different if his parents hadn't encouraged him to go into the Airforce – but said he wouldn't change anything now. He planned how he would spend the second half of his life and 'just slid into it' and 'never looked back'. His advice to others approaching retirement years is to think about what you've always wanted to do but haven't; he believes that this stage of life offers people the greatest opportunity to do those things. In his view it's not about money - you need enough to live on of course; it's about having the widest possible perspective on life, helping others, and living life with purpose.

JOY

For many years, Joy looked forward to her retirement. Her two primary interests, music and art, had taken a back seat during her very busy life raising a family and she worked almost full time until her late fifties.

While the children were growing up, Joy and her late husband operated a five-acre strawberry farm in Levin for many years. This in itself was a full-time job managing staff, packing strawberries, handling the administration, and operating the retail outlet. After the strawberry business closed down, she worked full time in local businesses and teaching, as well as running stock on the property. Even after the children left home, she spent a considerable amount of time looking after grand children while their parents worked.

Joy has always loved the outdoors, and in her fifties managed to make time for tramping, running, race walking, and volunteered with the local Search and Rescue Team. She joined the Levin joggers where she ran and race-walked several half marathons and took part in many long relay runs such as the 'Around the Mountains' and 'Coast to Coast' runs across the lower North Island. After retiring from full time work, she started attending a local dance group and learned sequence dancing, which she found she had a natural affinity for from her musical background. After a few year's dancing she met a new dance partner, David, at the group and they attended dances two or three times a week around the Horowhenua/Wellington region.

Several years later, she accepted David's proposal to marry and moved onto his farm in Reikorangi. She packed up and sold her farm and moved along with her goat, two ponies and some peacocks. Joy and David ran a retreat on the farm for several years where small groups stayed for weekends and holidays to experience rural life. In addition, they bred pedigree Highland cattle with new calves being born annually. A few years ago, the workload of the retreat and cattle breeding had lessened. This presented her with a wonderful opportunity to put some time into her old interests of music and art, as well as her interest in Japanese, while still maintaining a good connection with the land and the outdoors. The farm has a bush clad stream running through it which reminds her of her childhood home in Gracefield, Lower Hutt; she disappears, sometimes for a couple of hours, exploring the stream and bush.

Although, due to a heart condition, her half marathon days are over, Joy likes to get active by attending weekly Zumba classes where she pushes herself until she needs to sit and take a break. She also takes every opportunity to walk on the local streets, tracks, and beaches, although the hills do slow her down now. After twenty years David and Joy still attend the sequence dance groups twice a week and travel to weekend dances elsewhere in the region. These provide an opportunity to socialise with nice people in an atmosphere of music and laughter as well as physical exercise. Most importantly, Joy now has time to play her piano accordion. She started playing in her teens when she bought a second-hand accordion she spotted for sale. At the time, she couldn't read music, but had watched people play this instrument, recognised it was easily transportable, and learning to play it seemed like a challenge. Joy found a local music teacher and starting from scratch learned how to play the accordion.   Her music teacher conducted a piano accordion orchestra, which Joy soon joined, playing regularly in the Hutt Valley and in Wellington, often in public gardens and concert venues to raise money for charity.

On the farm David built Joy a large music and art studio where she spends relaxing time practising her accordion. As accordion orchestras are now a thing of the past, Joy took on the challenge of playing in front of other people by initially joining a local music group which met monthly. She was the only accordionist as most people played guitars, but she found it a good experience. She has recently joined a local Country Music Club where she plays to a larger audience. About two years ago she also joined the Kapiti Organ and Keyboard Club where she plays as the only accordionist and received a very warm welcome.

Joy's interest in art started early. At high school she enjoyed art more than any other subject; she particularly loved drawing. In her third form at high school, Joy's artwork featured in a display and a photograph of it was reported in the newspaper. In the fourth form she came top of the school in art and won the school prize – a book and a box of paints she still has to this day.

On leaving school Joy initially started work as a wage clerk, where she worked for three years before securing a job in Wellington as a Ticket Writer in a large department store. Meanwhile she attended art classes three-four nights a week to study still-life, life classes with models, portrait, typography and fashion drawing. It wasn't long before Joy secured a job in an advertising agency art studio working on layouts, lettering, printing, drawing, and paste-ups. In those days most of the signage, newspaper advertisements and illustrations were done by hand by artists. Although Joy enjoyed this work, she still held onto her desire to be a freestyle artist, painting in colour for her own pleasure.

Later in life after the family had grown, Joy worked again as an artist for a local newspaper, carton factory, textile print designer, and was self-employed as a Sign Writer for a while. Now she has moved to Reikorangi, she likes to spend time in her art studio painting in oils, water colour, and acrylics. She just enjoys creating art works either alone or with friends without the pressure of a commercial artist.

In her early fifties, with more spare time Joy looked for an opportunity to learn something new. A one-year 'Japanese for Beginners' class was offered at the local Library and this appealed to her, so she registered to attend. Joy enjoyed the class so much she repeated the course the following year and purchased Japanese books from the bookshop and began teaching herself the language as well. When Joy visited her elderly relatives in Wellington, she took the opportunity to meet the people at the Japanese Society and joined in the conversational class. Joy describes the atmosphere at the Society as being 'casual and easy' and she really appreciated the experience. As they say in life, one thing leads to another. In this case, the teacher who taught Japanese at the local High School in Levin moved on, and Joy was asked to facilitate the beginner's class for the students. Reluctantly

Joy took on the role as a temporary measure, but discovered she enjoyed the job and taught Japanese at the High School and the Intermediate School for the next few years.

In 1997, when a group from the Japanese Society hosted by Sakai (Wellington's sister city in Japan) went to Japan, Joy joined them and had a wonderful experience. Soon after, a trip to Japan was organised by Levin Intermediate School. Joy stayed on in Japan and assisted with this group of students as she had earlier taught them Japanese. Most of these students had never been overseas before so it was a significant cultural shift in every way – environment, food, language etc., from what they were accustomed to. The expedition was enjoyable, successful and memorable. When the children returned home, Joy stayed on in Japan to make the most of this once-in-a lifetime opportunity. Travelling solo, with nothing more than a backpack, she bravely explored the four main islands in Japan, often staying in youth hostels. Between October 1997 and March 1998, Joy trekked from region to region experiencing both snow and cherry blossom as the seasons changed from place to place. She recalls it being the 'Year of the Tiger', and for Joy a fabulous cultural experience. Returning to New Zealand Joy commenced and completed a Diploma in Japanese Studies.

Later life provides us with the freedom of choice; to learn new things, fulfil long nurtured ambitions, establish new routines, focus our time and our energy on the things we want to do, and spend time with people we like, love and appreciate. From Joy's perspective there is 'so much to see and do' and later life presents the opportunity to 'do the things you had put aside while you were working and raising your family'.

The studio is her special place where she can paint or play the piano accordion to her hearts content without time restrictions. Joy believes 'it's never too late to learn'. In fact, reflecting back on her life, she said she has found it easier to learn as an adult. At the time of writing she is attending two local six-week long art classes 'Watercolour' and 'Being Creative'. She enjoys the freedom to experiment and paints purely for pleasure.

Music plays a big part in Joy's life now. She owns five piano accordions, all with different capacities and sounds, including a big full-sized accordion and an older white one she picked up for $200. She bought another Titano - a lighter weight accordion, after she had surgery as it was hard to lift her old heavier accordion and therefore couldn't play it easily. Joy plays most days, not because she has to, but because she wants to. Her repertoire includes tangos, marches, popular and classical music. She loves challenging herself and taking things to the next level so chooses harder pieces of music than she did in the past.

Joy with her accordion on the farm in Reikorangi

Joy at home in Reikorangi

Joy, who is now in her 70's, lives a full and active life. She and David are proficient ballroom and sequence dancers, and she enjoys her hobbies, activities, and exercise groups, and supporting her husband's interests. Even with the workload of running a farm and keeping the property in order, there is always time for enjoying the outdoor life and being with family and friends.

Joy at home with a grandchild and her pets

OWEN TREVOR SMITH

Trevor was born in Wellington in 1947. His birth was extra special for his parents as he was the first 'live' child to be born in the family. Trevor grew up in Paekakariki, a small coastal town in the south-western North Island of New Zealand, 40 kilometres north of the capital city Wellington. It's an idyllic setting in which to spend a childhood with the beach and the Tasman Sea on one side of the township and the Akatarawa Ranges on the other. He and his younger sister attended the small village school Paekakariki Primary School, and later went to high school at Kapiti College, ten kilometres further north in Raumati Beach. On leaving school Trevor majored in psychology and education at Victoria University in Wellington as he was keen to work at the Ministry of Education as a child psychologist. Regrettably, his hopes for this career were dashed when his mentor left the organisation and the system changed, leaving him at a bit of a loose end when he graduated.

Undeterred, Trevor and a good friend decided to take a gap year from their studies while they considered their options. At the time (1968), the Forestry Department in New Zealand were allocating blocks of land to possum trappers to mitigate the damage the marsupials were causing to the forests. Neither of the lads knew anything about possum trapping, but it seemed like an adventure to them. Fired up with enthusiasm, they attended a training course where they learned how to do the job safely, including how to trap, skin, store and sell the possum skins. They did their research on the subject and submitted a successful bid for a block of land in Awakino - a small rustic settlement off the beaten track, north of New Plymouth. Before embarking on their adventure, they bought a dog named 'Blue' from the Society for the Prevention of Cruelty to Animals (SPCA) in Newtown Wellington, anticipating the dog would help them find the possums in the thick bush. For 18 months the youngsters lived in a shepherd's hut on a farm in Awakino, setting a line of traps one day, checking them the next, and resetting another line of traps. Every month a buyer came to meet the trappers at the Awakino Tavern to inspect the skins and offer a price. Although Blue proved to be useless at her assigned task, it was a lucrative business for the lads. In those days the going rate was $3 for a brown skin and $5 for a silver skin, with their level of income dependent on their level of motivation. Trevor recalls their adventure as being "a big learning curve and lots of fun", but it wasn't the career he was looking for.

Returning to Wellington, Trevor became the Personnel Officer at the Ford Motor Company, in Seaview, in the Hutt Valley. In this role he recruited workers for the various factory departments and managed the advertising for executive positions. As a side-line he wrote the copy for company advertisements and also the Christmas Cards. Ford Motor Company was a major employer in the Wellington region; there were hundreds of staff and it was a great opportunity to apply what he'd learned at University. During this period, Trevor shared a flat in Wellington with a friend from University who was completing a computer programming course at the local polytechnic. Discussions in the flat invariably centred on various aspects of computer programming and the problem solving associated with it.

These conversations sparked Trevor's interest in the subject, and subsequently he registered for and completed a course in computer programming and systems analysis at Wellington Polytechnic. This qualification ultimately became the catalyst for the change in the direction of his career.

When he completed the course in the early 1970's, Trevor secured his first computer programming role with Government Computer Services (GCS), where he met his wife Jane. In 1976, the Wanganui Computer Centre opened and both Trevor and his wife relocated to Wanganui where Trevor was to lead the team developing a series of systems for the NZ Police. This purpose-built 'state of the art' facility employed 80 people, and Trevor regularly took dignitaries for a tour around the premises. It was set up to manage the 'Law Enforcement System' – effectively the operational management and historical information needed by the justice sector agencies, specifically the Police, Justice, Land Transport and later the Serious Fraud Office. At the time, the Minister of Police, Allan McCready described it as 'the most significant crime-fighting weapon ever brought to bear in New Zealand'. The Police Team developed systems for fingerprint analysis, Computer Assisted Despatch of resources, computerised incident reporting, stolen property, and vehicles and persons of interest. The work was stimulating, the technology and software were world-leading and as Trevor said, 'you really felt you were doing some good'.

Trevor was lured away from the Wanganui Computer Centre by an old friend who was working in England. The timing was perfect as Information Technology was really taking off in the business world and skilled computer programmers were in short supply. Both Trevor and Jane were offered programming contracts with a Hewlett Packard recruitment agency in the United Kingdom. It was a great opportunity to gain international experience, earn a respectable income, and a chance to explore Europe. The idea was to work a year and then the couple would take six months off to travel. In England, Trevor's first contract was with Blackman Martin, a small engineering company in Swindon headed up by Lord Robert. Not only was Trevor introduced to the English aristocracy, it was here that he designed and programmed a prototype of the first 'spreadsheet'. When this contract ended, he accepted a one-year contract in Hamelin, Germany – the 'Pied Piper' town. Trevor didn't speak German, but he quickly set to work to learn the language and got to know and appreciate the culture of the country whilst living and working in Hamelin. Two years later, the couple had saved enough money to tour Europe for 12 months in a campervan. Then they spent an additional 10 months touring the United States in a Dodge V8 Custom Van. Trevor said this was a 'fantastic experience' as they had the time to really explore and not just do a brief tourist visit. It was 'great fun'. At the end of their extended holiday, the couple returned home to New Zealand, but sadly the marriage ended. Back in Wellington, Trevor secured a job with the New Zealand Defence Force where he developed two separate systems – a depot and retail supply system and an accounting management system.

He undertook one more contract in England, where he and a friend combined their resources and bought 'Adastra', a 41-foot ocean going yacht. The pair spent a year kitting it out before setting off on an adventure of a lifetime. With a small team of four to five people, they sailed the yacht to the Canaries, Spain, then across the Atlantic Ocean to Brazil to experience the famous carnival festival celebrated in Salvador in the Brazilian state of Bahia.

Owen Trevor Smith at the helm of the Adastra

Although the carnival event officially lasts for six days, Trevor stayed for six weeks. Parting with the yacht, he travelled on to Peru to visit Cusco, a UNESCO World Heritage Site and the Inca citadel at Machu Picchu. By this time Trevor was 40 – adventurous at any age!

Returning to the southern hemisphere, Trevor completed a couple of major projects for the New Zealand Broadcasting

Corporation. One was a redevelopment of the Payroll system and the other an Advertising Management system for the 'New Zealand Listener', the iconic weekly magazine that covered the political, cultural and literary life of the nation. Interestingly, as a 21-year-old student, Trevor had written a short story called 'Boss' that had been published in the Listener years before. He was paid $20 for his story, and still has a copy of that edition of the magazine, which at the time cost the reader 10 cents! As providence would have it, here he was now working for the magazine that had published his first story. Fortuitously, while working at the Broadcasting Corporation, Trevor met and married his second wife Gail.

Always adventurous, open to learning new skills and new experiences, Trevor has never been afraid to change direction. In his early fifties he decided to take time off from his computer programming career to pursue other interests. Along with his wife Gail and their son Aidan, they moved to Queensland, Australia, purchased a franchise and started a business called the 'Whacky Fun Factory'. In this business he purchased large gumball vending machines, installed them in shopping malls throughout the state and serviced them when required. Within two years he had 30 vending machines operating in various locations. Although the business was successful, it was no longer challenging requiring only two day's work per fortnight to service the machines. Eventually Trevor was enticed back into computer programming when Unisys offered him a job in Switzerland. It was a great opportunity for the whole family and Trevor could already speak the language, so he accepted the position, sold his business and the whole family relocated to Zurich to begin what became a two-year adventure. When both Gail and

Trevor's parents became ill, Trevor secured a job with Unisys in New Zealand and the family came home to care for them.

Trevor retired from his full-time job with Unisys when he was 71 years of age. Now in semi-retirement he channels his energy into pursuing his interests. He continues to seek opportunities to learn and take on challenging projects. Throughout his adult life he had written several short stories in his spare time and is now focusing more on this activity. In 2015, Trevor published a collection of stories in a book entitled 'Seven Roads To Travel'. In this book he has taken the time and care to preface each story, sharing his inspiration and/or personal experience for writing it, which is very insightful for the reader. 'Boss', his story that was originally published in the Listener, is included in this collection. The same year he also published 'The Day Bonny Blue Raced For The Cup' – it's an epic 66-verse poem in the style of legendary Australian 'bush' poets' Andrew 'Banjo' Patterson and Henry Lawson.

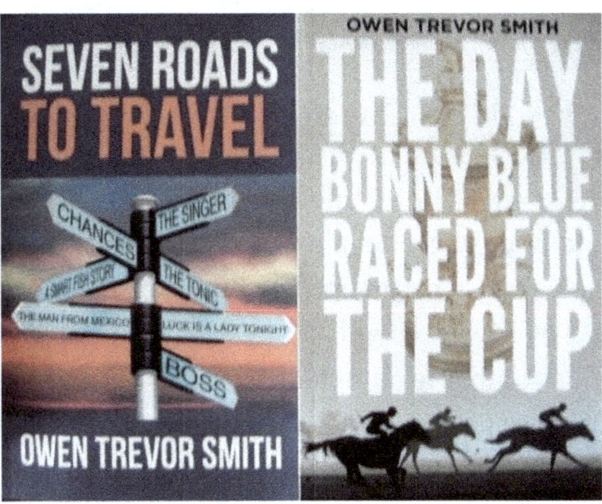

Trevor's third book, 'Lindisfarne – Fury of the Northmen' - a historical work of fiction set in the Viking era, was published in 2018. His fourth book, 'The Pharaoh of Venice', a gripping story set in the dangerous world of international intrigue, was published in 2019. Trevor's adventurous nature, and imaginative thought-provoking style of writing, covers a broad range of genres. A member of the local writers' group, he is an inspiration to budding writers.

Trevor, now in his 72nd year, is currently working on several projects. He has spent the last four months updating and rewriting a computer game he created for his son several years ago and is also developing sequels for his two novels. Over the years he has maintained his social and professional networks and is still friends today with the people he studied with in his youth. He continues to lead a full and exciting life, maximising opportunities as they present themselves.

Trevor's books can be purchased online from
www.bookdepository.com and
www.amazon.com/s?k=owen+trevor+smith

He wrote this poem some time ago and it's a privilege to
share it with you. It relates to any great endeavour such as
the journey authors undertake.

Says the one who is wise:
'Your alarm at the size
Of the mountain to climb
Is a waste of your time.
You should focus instead
On the rock just ahead.'

THOMAS MURRAY WILSON

Murray, the eldest of seven children, was born in 1944 in the farming district of Browns in Invercargill. He was named after an Uncle, Thomas Murray, who was killed overseas during the war but is fondly known as Murray. The family owned a farm where they raised sheep and pigs and managed a small herd of dairy cows. Although his Dad was a good farmer, he was an alcoholic and was often away from home, sometimes for days at a time, so Murray, as the eldest, had to help his Mum manage the farm, milk the cows and raise the family. Given his responsibilities on the farm, Murray could only attend school intermittently and therefore he struggled with his schoolwork. Times were tough. It wasn't a happy childhood. Murray left school when he was 15 to work on the farm full-time, but eventually the farm had to be sold. The family moved 161 kilometres north to a smaller farm in Roxburgh, Central Otago where Murray secured a job in a local orchard, although he continued to work on the family farm helping with the lambing and the haymaking. Five years later, Murray's brothers and sisters were growing up too, so the farm was sold, and his parents bought a family home in Roxburgh. Shortly afterwards his Dad left home and went bush on the West Coast of the South Island. Recalling his early life Murray said he felt as if he lived under a dark cloud until he was 20 years old and vowed that he would never get drunk.

When the family moved into their new home in Roxburgh, Murray's responsibilities diminished. At 20 years of age he decided it was time for a change. Together with a friend they booked their passage on the 'Fair Sky' and set off on their big 'OE' (overseas experience) to Australia. Murray recalls the excitement of embarking on an overseas adventure and having the freedom to do so, just like other young New Zealanders. Arriving in Brisbane they picked up odd jobs for the first two to three months and then Murray got a job with a pest control contractor, killing ants in Brisbane and Toowoomba. He stayed with a family in Gatton, which is a small country town on the Gold Coast in Queensland. Here in addition to his pest control work, he also managed to pick up a job painting. For Murray this was the beginning of a whole new life where he could spread his wings.

Two years sped by. Murray missed his family. Feeling a sense of responsibility, he returned to Roxburgh to spend time with them. He went back to work for his previous employer at the orchard and this is where he met Deanne, his partner in life. At the time Deanne was undertaking a horticultural course at Massey University. As part of the course she had to work on-site to gain practical experience in her field. Telling the story Murray said they met 'up a cherry tree' and as they worked long hours together picking the fruit and packing it in the packhouse every day, they got to know each other really well. It was a perfect match. Three months later the couple got married in Auckland where Deanne's family lived at the time. Murray and Deanne began their married life in a cottage on the orchard in Roxburgh and this is where Austin, the first of their three children was born. Shortly after, Murray was offered a job managing an orchard in Clyde. It was a great opportunity, so the family relocated 46 kilometres north, settled in Clyde and this is where Vicky, their second child was born. Unfortunately, within six months the owner sold the orchard which left Murray and Deanne and their young family in a bit of a predicament.

By this time Murray's mother and siblings had moved to Dunedin and Murray and Deanne joined them. In Dunedin Murray joined The Church of Jesus Christ of Latter-Day Saints in which Deanne had been raised, and both remain active members to this day. Murray initially secured a job as a storeman with Bonaire Fridges and Freezers and he and Deanne managed to get a state house in Mosgiel, a suburb in Dunedin, where Jared, their third child was born.

Both of Murray's brothers were working in engineering and Murray became interested in this type of work. When he took a job with Dunedin Engineering, he was given the opportunity to work overtime hours on the floor with 30-40 tradesmen who were cutting and rolling metal for the hydro jobs they were working on. Murray not only enjoyed the work; he was good at it. It wasn't long before the men he worked with encouraged him to complete an adult apprenticeship with the support of the firm. At first Murray was reluctant as he'd had limited schooling and this harsh experience had knocked his confidence - but Deanne encouraged and supported her husband to take on the challenge. Murray, who was 32 years old at the time, was one of five men who took on an adult apprenticeship. He had to travel from Dunedin in the South Island to Auckland in the North Island to complete his block course training sessions over a three-year period. As Murray is dyslexic, he found the training extremely challenging, but he persevered, got help with his reading and qualified as a Boilermaker in 1979.

Murray said he's "always been thankful" to the men and Deanne who encouraged and supported him.

Deanne's father and siblings lived in Auckland. When Murray qualified as a boilermaker, he, Deanne and their three children moved to Auckland to spend time near them. Murray secured a job pile drilling the structural foundations for large buildings with Gilbert Hadfield Piling (GHP). He worked for this firm for six-seven years while his three children were growing up. Regrettably New Zealand experienced a downturn in the economy, which impacted on employment opportunities. As a result, GHP had to lay off most of their workers. Murray then began working for Brian Perry Engineering, but after three or four years this company was also drastically downsized when it was taken over by Fletchers

While Murray considered his options, quite by chance he heard a top hypnotherapist, Brian Head, talk on a radio chat show. Hypnotherapy is an alternative practice that aims to effect emotional and mental healing by accessing the subconscious to work through past traumas that can get lodged there. Hypnosis and guided imagery are used to create a state of focused attention to help individuals deal with a variety of concerns and issues. The hypnotherapist was running courses in Auckland for people who wanted to help themselves using this process. Intrigued, Murray rang the hypnotherapist and booked himself on the training course. He enjoyed the training session so much that over time he underwent further training, completed the practical tests, became a practitioner and started his own hypnotherapy practice. During this period Murray also became a Reiki practitioner, as did his sister and a cousin, recognising they could channel universally available healing energy through their hands.

For the next 17-18 years Murray worked for Visor Distributors in Auckland doing light engineering work such as fitting air spoilers on trucks and windscreens on buses. During this period, he operated his part-time wellness business practicing hypnotherapy and reiki in the evenings and on the weekends. Over the years the couple's three children had grown up and there was a pull to return to the South Island to spend time near Murray's parents and siblings. Deanne and Murray bought a five acre lifestyle block in Invercargill, more than 1,000 kilometres from Auckland, built a Lockwood home on the section and spent the next six years planting and tending shelter and fruit trees and developing their vegetable and flower gardens, all as closely as possible to Permaculture principles (eco-friendly sustainable living). Murray took a light engineering job for the 12 months leading up to his 65th birthday. They loved the lifestyle in Invercargill but missed their adult children who were then living in the North Island which seemed a long way away.

After six years in Invercargill, under pressure by two of their children to be more accessible in case they needed help, they decided the time was right to relocate. They sold their home and moved to Levin in the Horowhenua to be closer to their daughter who lived just down the road in Otaki. Levin is the largest town in the Horowhenua and a service centre for the surrounding rural area where there are several market gardens. The town had everything Deanne and Murray wanted so they bought a house with a large garden where they live to this day.

At the time of writing Murray and Deanne have been married for 52 years. In Murray's words 'it's a good match' – a true partnership. The couple spend a lot of time gardening, which they both enjoy, and are active members of their church. Murray still practices hypnotherapy and reiki for people who need it. He volunteers for the local Senior Citizens group, is on the committee that plans activities and drives, and does some of the repairs and maintenance on the Senior Citizens' (also ageing) building, fixtures and fittings.

Murray said he's "blessed with good health" and appreciates his life experience has been really helpful to him and, as a result, enables him to help others. He and Deanne regularly visit 10-12 households in their community some of whose occupants are housebound, while others are young couples coming to terms with the everyday challenges, we all face in some form. He said they are like grandparents to these young people; so, as well as making scheduled visits, they call on them 'out of the blue' just to show they care, as there is 'nothing like face-to-face contact'.

Reflecting on life, family has always been important to Murray and Deanne. He says they have become much more aware of how important their family is as they get older. Now aged 75, Murray recently renewed his driver's licence. As he and Deanne have retired, they are able to spend much more time travelling to visiting family and friends in New Zealand and in Australia. Their youngest son Jared married Gosia who is Polish, and the couple have two children. At the time of writing this family are spending a year in Poland to be closer to Gosia's parents. They see it as an opportunity to enjoy a shared family and cultural experience while they can. Murray and Deanne keep in touch with them once a week on skype. Everyone has chipped in to help – Vicky and her partner Terry are looking after her brother's home in Melbourne while he, Gosia, and their children Rosa and Roman are away, and Murray has inherited a dog, Jasper, spoilt but lovable and becoming more spoilt, for 12 months.

When asked for a favourite quote, Murray came up with two short ones. The first from David O' McKay:

"The most important work you will ever do will be within the walls of your own home".

The second, of unknown provenance:

"Family – We may not have it all together, but together we have it all".

Deanne and Murray in their garden

KILIAN de LACY

Kilian was born in Wellington in the early 1940's. She was the second of six children born over a 17-year period, and the older daughter, so there was a considerable age gap between the oldest and the youngest of her siblings. Her parents were devout Catholics. It's the faith in which the children were raised where the priests and nuns were regarded as the voice of God.

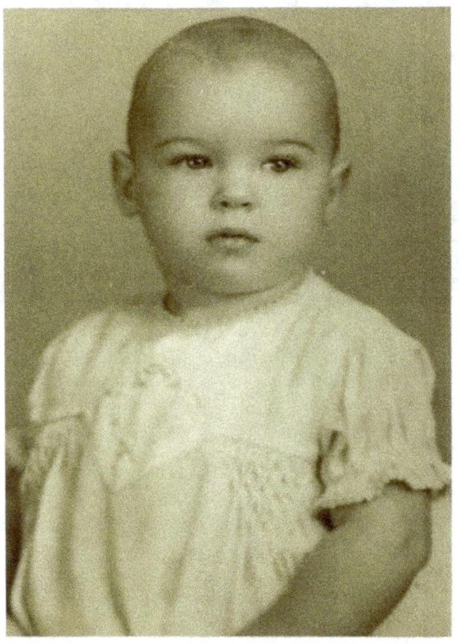

Kilian as a baby

Throughout most of her primary and high school education Kilian attended Catholic Schools where she was taught by the nuns – colloquially known as the 'Black Joes' – the Sisters of St Joseph - as they wore black habits. Two of the schools she attended were boarding schools for girls – one in Otaki where there were only 12 boarders, and the other was Sacred Heart Convent in Whanganui. The nuns were thorough in the teachings of the church where the students were strongly encouraged to be altruistic and do what God wanted, or they'd go straight to hell when they died. This doctrine was firmly endorsed in Kilian's family. The ultimate vocation for a young woman was to become a nun, with an assurance that choosing this path to godliness would guarantee one would go straight to heaven when one died, and in the meantime the family would be blessed.

Kilian was a bright student, enjoyed school and embraced the faith she grew up with. As a teenager she wanted to be a surgeon but wrestled with the question 'What if God doesn't want me to be a surgeon? Does he want me to be a nun?' She really did not want to go to hell in the end. Talking it over, she was told that 'If you really want to know if God wants you in a convent, you should try it and see what happens. If you are accepted to take your vows, then God wants you'. So, she thought she had better test this statement. In 1959, aged 17, almost straight from school, Kilian was admitted to the Home of Compassion in Wellington, taking the first formal step as a postulant - a 'seeker', where she learned the ropes from the longer serving nuns. Apart from her family life, she had had limited life experience outside of school.

Over the next few years Kilian was called to take her vows, including the vow of obedience, and bowed to the inevitable. She trained as a Registered Nurse and topped the Dominion in the exam (for which she was sent to Broken Hill, Australia – presumably to ensure she did not become proud of her success) and became a qualified Radiographer. She had joined an active order that worked in the community and, as with the other nuns, she also did her fair share of the chores in the convent.

Kilian at Broken Hill 1968-1975

As with any organisation, there is a governing system, with the Superiors making the decisions in a convent. Kilian is a practical person and had so much to give, but often felt restricted. Highly intelligent, she asked for stretch assignments and questioned the status quo, an awkward situation given the vow of obedience. As the years passed, she did a lot of soul searching as she found it more and more difficult to fit the mould and wanted to be who she was. She found it difficult to talk about her unrest as she felt she was being untrue to her vocation.

Kilian had been a nun for 25 years when she was permitted to go to a Benedictine contemplative order in Pennant Hills in Australia for what is now known as a sabbatical. The idea was that the contemplative order would give her the space to 'just be' - to pray, sing, and participate in the life of the community. In this environment there were no expectations of Kilian and she fitted into the monastic life of prayer and periods of silence and solitude, an experience she cherished. She was initially given nine months at the Abbey, but within three months was ordered to return to New Zealand. There, she was instructed to participate in a refresher course in Timaru, then agreed to facilitate a spirituality course for another group for six weeks, after which she was allowed to return to the convent in Australia for a further three months.

Kilian in the new look habit of the 1980's

In 1988, the whole order took part in a retreat (an eight-day withdrawal from normal duties to renew one's commitment to God). During the retreat Kilian had a dream. In it she was in a maternity ward, a situation she hadn't worked in for 20 years. Two young women undergoing miscarriage were put into her care. On looking at one, she noticed the patient's eyes glazing over and her skin turning grey. Just as she went to press the emergency button to get help – Kilian woke up. She shared her dream with her Sisters, still mystified as to its meaning. The Superior General, the ultimate authority in the Sisterhood, agreed that Kilian could get help from a non-Catholic woman outside of the 'system'. Kilian met with a psychologist and described her dream and her difficulty in applying it to anything in particular. The psychologist asked, "Did you think of applying it to yourself?" Talking this through, Kilian realised that she had been soul searching and grieving to be herself for years and now knew after 30 years as a nun that she didn't have to stay. She made the decision to leave the order and applied for a dispensation from Rome, then stayed in the convent and wore her habit for a further two months until the details were finalised. During this time, the other nuns were very supportive.

As nuns relinquish personal possessions, Kilian, then 47 years old, would have been left with nothing, but it is the rule of the Church that a religious order must ensure the wellbeing of Sisters who leave their ranks like this, so she was not destitute. Her sister was very encouraging and helped her to find somewhere to live, open a bank account, apply for an IRD number (Tax details) and insurance – things she had never had or needed in the past, and she provided some clothes. Kilian's first paid job was as a relieving nurse at

Arohata prison in Porirua and she bought herself a sewing machine. She signed up with a nursing bureau in the Hutt Valley and sought work as a Radiographer. Kilian worked after hours two nights a week (one as a nurse and one as a radiographer) at Wellington After Hours Centre and was Night Nurse in Charge at the Home of Compassion on the weekends. She later became the Hotel Housekeeper at the Terrace Regency Hotel in Wellington where, for the first time, she had the responsibility for hiring and firing staff. Although Kilian had chosen to leave the convent, she never lost her faith and remained very involved with the Catholic Church. For recreation she joined the Gilbert & Sullivan Society and the local Opera Company.

Kilian in "Faust" 1990

Kilian with her siblings in 1990

Three years after leaving the nunnery, Kilian met Bruce when she responded to an advertisement in the 'Personal' column in the Evening Post. Kilian recalls their first date was at the 'Old Flame' restaurant in Petone. In 1991, within a year of meeting each other, they were married.

Kilian and Bruce on their wedding day

For the first six years they lived in Lyall Bay, Wellington, then for the next 18 years moved to Porirua. During this time Kilian began to experience knee problems and, as a result, had to give up nursing. Leveraging her strengths, she took on clerical roles with New Zealand on Air, the Cancer Society, the Bible Society in Wellington, and a senior supporting role at Bowen Hospital. Regrettably, in 2001, Bruce became quite ill and at 63 years of age had to resign from his job with New Zealand Qualifications Authority (NZQA). Kilian, then aged 60, left work to look after him.

Throughout her married life Kilian kept her faith and took an active role in the parish and with the Samoan congregation within this community. She played the organ in church and still enjoyed singing. When the Archdiocese of Wellington was looking for lay people to work in the parishes, Kilian expressed an interest. She completed a Diploma in Pastoral Ministry through the Wellington Catholic Education Centre and was one of the first to graduate with this qualification in 2005. In 2007 she was appointed as the Senior Catholic Prison Chaplain, a national role she held for three years supporting a network of Chaplains working in this field. Kilian also became a tutor for the Catholic Institute in Spirituality in Pastoral Ministry. By 1999, her knees were showing the effects of, as she put it, 'all that kneeling and genuflecting in church' and she underwent surgery to have both knees replaced.

During these years, at a time when many people reduce their commitments and consider semi-retirement, Kilian joined Grey Power in 2001, and quickly worked her way through the ranks. She was the President of the Mana/Tawa Branch of

Grey Power and later was appointed as a Zone Director. At the time of writing Kilian is the Representative for Zone 4 on the National Board for Grey Power. While in Grey Power, she was invited to join the Health and Disability Commission's Consumer Advisory Group for Disability, a role she maintains to this day. She really enjoys lobbying for people over the age of 50, an interest she shares with her husband Bruce who has worked with her in various roles within the organisation.

Looking to the future, Bruce and Kilian knew when it was time to downsize and move out of the city. They put their house on the market, bought a section in the Horowhenua and built an eco-tech, single story, low maintenance, modular home, close to Levin's town centre.   They anticipated what they will need in later life and have future-proofed their home. Their house is designed so that it is not too small for two people, and not too big for one. It has wider doorways, ramps and a deck, easy access to an outdoor undercover area where their washing can dry in the fresh air, and wet floors in the bathrooms. Talking it over Kilian says, 'it was a very practical decision'. As a couple they intend to enjoy their independence for as long as they possibly can.

Since they relocated to the Horowhenua (four years ago), Kilian and Bruce have made a whole new circle of friends and the Catholic parish has been 'very welcoming'. Kilian is the Chair of the Pastoral Team in Levin, visits the sick and administers holy communion, and reads in church. She continues to draw on her nursing background in the community, ensuring people get the spiritual and medical help they need in a timely manner.   As the Zone Representative for Grey Power, Kilian was a key contributor in the development of the Ministry of Social Welfare's 'Better Later Life' Strategy and helped initiate front office improvements in the Ministry's local branches, improving the ambience and privacy for those using these services. Kilian is a giver. She is always up for a challenge and constantly looks for ways to contribute. In Kilian's down-to-earth words she says she 'just keeps on keeping on'.

Kilian and Bruce recently celebrated their 28th Wedding Anniversary. They have become part of the fabric of the community in the Horowhenua and participate in as many activities as health allows. Furthermore, they maintain a strong interest and involvement in the bigger issues in New Zealand, especially spiritual and social development in the wider community.

In 2007, Kilian wrote a book about her life called 'God Must Be Crazy'. Although the book is no longer in print it is available in libraries in New Zealand.

TED AND ALISON KOIA

Ted and Alison were born and raised in Whakatane a coastal town situated in the eastern Bay of Plenty. Whakatane is known as one of the sunniest towns in New Zealand and Maori pa sites in this area date back to the first Polynesian settlements. Ted, who is part-Maori, was one of seven children, and Alison has four siblings. The couple have lived here all their lives. They met at Magnus Lennie where they worked; Ted was a motor mechanic and Alison worked in the office. Alison recalls that Ted was so shy he asked the other girls in the office to ask Alison to go out with him. It was love at first sight. They married in 1961 when Ted was 20 and Alison was only 17 years old - as Alison said 'everyone got married young in those days, my sisters were married when they were in their teens'.

Ted and Alison in 1964 - the year Ted toured Australia with his rugby team.

When Ted secured a job at the Tasman Mill, the couple moved to Kawerau. It was a good well-paid job, that came with a raft of additional allowances such as 'heat money' and rental accommodation provided by the Mill. Alison was able to get a transfer in her job to Lenny Morgan Motors in Kawarau. They worked hard as a team in those early years and Ted took advantage of all the overtime opportunities that were on offer to help set the couple up for the future, whilst at the same time becoming part of the wider community. In 1966, their family expanded with the arrival of Tony, their first child.

Ted and Alison had been married for 10 years when they made the decision to sell their car and buy a part-time mobile repair business in 1972. They renamed the business 'Koia Motors'. The same year Grant, their second child was born, followed 10 months later by their third son, Paul. In the coming years Ted and Alison worked incredibly hard to build their business up repairing all kinds of tools such as chainsaws and other forestry equipment. Word got around and within four years the business had expanded so much that they bought a section and built their own shop and their family home. To this day they remember how proud Ted's Dad was when he visited them and saw the family name 'Koia' on the building.

Koia Motors

Although Ted and Alison worked hard together to grow their business, there was always plenty of time to spend with the family. They especially enjoyed their annual camping holidays with the family at Te Kaha where they cooked their food on fires outside.

Ted and Alison's three children at the beach

During these years Ted enjoyed cycling and long-distance running. Between 1964 - 1973 he ran in the annual mountain race up Mount Edgecumbe (also known as Putauaki), initially achieving third place and his personal best was second place.

In 1973 Ted came second in the Mountain race
– pictured here with his Mum and Dad

Furthermore, he was a children's rugby coach, an active member of the local Lions Club, and also played in the 'Metro Golden Airs' band.

By 1979, Ted and Alison were keen to travel with the family and experience life in Europe. They sold some of their belongings, stored what they wanted to keep and rented out the shop and their family home. In April that year, they set off – first stop Wellington, where they enrolled their three children in Correspondence School. At the time the children were aged 13, six and five years old and Tony, the eldest was due to start High School. Armed with six months' supply of schoolwork the family set off on a trip of a lifetime.

Arriving in London Ted and Alison bought a motorhome and spent the next 18 months travelling around Europe. During this time Alison home schooled the children. They spent their first winter overseas in Sweden where Ted planned to meet up with his contacts at the Husqvarna factory. As Ted was familiar with Husqvarna chainsaws and some of their other tools, they offered him a job at the factory and supported him to get a work permit. It was so cold in the campervan, the locals offered the family accommodation at a hotel, free of charge as it wasn't used in the winter months. It was a great opportunity and Ted and Alison were incredibly grateful. When a Dutch contingent arrived for Christmas, Ted dressed up as the English-speaking Santa and Grant, their middle son, dressed as an elf. It was their job to distribute presents to everyone. The family spent six months in Sweden before moving on to explore other countries. Reflecting back Alison said, 'it was a wonderful family experience'. In the evenings, the family would entertain themselves, often having their 'own little party'. Ted would play the ukulele and the children would use the jam spoons as drumsticks and sing along together. Picking up the mail enroute at the Poste Restante was another highlight, enabling them to keep in touch with the family back in New Zealand.

The family returned to New Zealand in September 1981 and the children settled back into school. Within a few months Ted and Alison started a new business in Whakatane – 'Chainsaws and Mowers'. Remembering Ted, and the quality of his work, many of his old customers came back to him and so this became a thriving business. Alison initially got a job in a furniture store but gave this job up to help Ted with their own business. A few years later the couple bought a boarding kennel for cats and dogs on a five-acre section where Alison looked after the animals for several years while Ted ran the repair business.

Ted took up rugby again but had to give this up when he had his first hip replacement at 44 years of age, and his other hip was replaced shortly afterwards. Over the next few years Ted had both knees replaced and major surgery on his shoulder. Although 'Chainsaws and Mowers' was a successful business Ted's health and wellbeing became a priority when he learned he had to have yet another hip replacement. It became clear that it was time to sell the business.

Ted was very highly regarded at Husqvarna, and when this company heard Ted was selling his business, they snapped him up to be a sales representative for them selling chainsaws and other tools of the trade. Ted was also able to provide training for his customers all over the country in how to safely use these tools. He loved this job and remained with this company until he was 68 years old - past the age he was entitled to universal government superannuation.

Meanwhile, Ted and Alison's three children grew up and left home, but everyone would come home for Christmas as there were approximately 100 or so cats and 50 or more dogs to look after at the boarding kennels over the holiday period. Alison said there came a time when they asked themselves "why are we doing this?" and realised it was time to put this business on the market and move on. When 'Chainsaws and Mowers' was sold, the furniture shop where Alison had previously worked (Meikle Brothers – later known as Smith City), invited her back and she worked for this company for 26 years. Thinking through the transition into retirement Alison gradually reduced her hours from full-time to part time hours over a three-year period, finally retiring from her job when she was 72 years old.

The next question was "what are we going to do now?" – after all both Ted and Alison had worked all of their lives. There really was no need to worry, as they lost no time making new plans for their future and putting them into place. The couple bought themselves a new home in Ohope, a beautiful beach settlement just six kilometres from Whakatane. Ted loves fishing so the location is perfect for him to pursue his hobby. At the time of writing Ted is 78 years of age. Now that he has retired, he has the time to play golf twice a week, which wasn't possible when he was working. Alison does Pilates twice a week, and volunteers for the charity Alzheimer's once a week where, as a companion, she takes members on outings for coffee and to pick strawberries. She keeps in touch with her friends and likes to catch up with them for lunch as often as possible. Both Ted and Alison play bowls socially – just for fun.

Ted and Alison are active members of the community they have been part of for most of their lives. Two of their three children live in the district and Tony, their eldest son lives just three hours' drive away in Auckland. Living in close proximity to their sons and their partners and their three grandchildren, means they are able to see them all on a regular basis.   Having said that, this couple have enthusiastically nurtured and retained their sense of adventure over the years. They budget and plan an overseas trip each year visiting various countries in Europe and Asia. In retirement they have courageously backpacked around Indonesia and explored the length and breadth of Vietnam on buses, trains and motorbikes. In 2019 they enjoyed a river cruise from Amsterdam to Budapest.

Ted and Alison wearing traditional Dutch costumes in Volendam, Holland

Ted and Alison are currently planning a trip to China. Now, instead of the camping holidays they used to enjoy when they were younger, they enjoy regular trips around New Zealand in their luxury caravan.

"It is not the years in your life, but the life in your years that counts" – Adlai Stevenson

ALASTAIR PAIN

Alastair was born in Auckland at the beginning of the Second World War. The family moved to Wellington when he was five years old, and this is where he went to school. Alastair describes his nuclear family, his parents and sister, as being 'really supportive' and 'loving in an adventurous and adaptive way'. He recalls his childhood as being filled with stories; poetry and music/song, in a home surrounded by books. Eric, his father, was a scientist graduating in chemistry, physics and maths, and Jenny, his mother, studied at Elam School of Fine Arts. Alastair said 'we were brought up with psychology, encouraged to explore widely, and pursue our passions, including interests in nature and the arts'. At age three, a week after his sister Kathryn was born, Alastair became a vegetarian following a traumatic experience when he visited the rail yard at Southdown Freezing Works where his Dad was a Chemist. This led to his interest in animal welfare and humanitarianism, values that are enduring in Alastair's life.

Upon leaving school Alastair studied Wool Classing and while working in a Napier wool store, he met Jan. After a four-year engagement, they married. Alastair went on to study Theology, trained as a counsellor and became a Methodist Minister. Eric Hames, a mentor, encouraged Alastair to take the challenge of a university education, which he did, studying Anthropology, English and Psychology at the University of Canterbury.

As newlyweds Alastair and Jan moved to Wellsford just inside the Northland boundary, where Alastair was the Methodist Minister. His ministry was based on what was known at the time as "the accepting love of Jesus". These were good and challenging times in a rural community. Alastair was interested in the practices at Ted Knoff's 'Wayside Chapel of the Cross' in Sydney, with its 'no strings attached ministry', and wanted to apply these principles in the Wellsford parish. Futuristic in this thinking, he provided opportunities for the community to come together in non-traditional ways, regardless of their beliefs, world views and personal circumstances, for fellowship and support both in and outside church and worship. In the 1960s, this philosophy was unconventional in rural New Zealand, and challenged the status quo. Alastair likes challenges and engages his heart and mind in everything he does. In 1967 he saw the need for a community project, was prepared to take the risks, set things up from scratch to give it a go, and was prepared to learn from the experience. Unfortunately, his idea for a 'no strings attached meeting place' which was widely supported by the Wellsford community, wasn't upheld by the Church, and therefore the community project couldn't go ahead without this approval. The decision clashed with Alastair's core values and sadly he resigned from his calling as a Methodist Minister.

Reading books like Nietzsche's 'Thus Spoke Zarathustra' and William Sargent's 'Battle for the Mind' sparked a changing viewpoint for Alastair and led to a different world view, in which the evidence necessary for scientific discoveries and truths became important. Through these changes Alastair remained true to his philosophy and commitment to animal rights. Mentors were generous in their support and creative challenges abounded. John Daniell of Wairere Station in the Wairapapa, was such a mentor. Alastair was 'Cowman/Gardener' at Wairere and after a particularly fortuitous sorting of the crutching's clip, it was John who advised Alastair to train as a Wool Classer. Years later with a graduate degree behind him, Alastair returned to his first love – agriculture and became the Education Officer with the Agricultural Training Council. A number of Regional Training Officers were subsequently appointed to promote, encourage and facilitate education and training for a life/career in horticulture and/or agriculture. Alastair recalls these were exciting times.

Meanwhile, Jan and Alastair opened a craft shop called 'New Zealand Craftworks' which was featured in 'Designscape' and was respected as "one of New Zealand's best for the 10 years of its life". Change being the only constant in life, Alastair took a role at 'The Management Centre' at the Wellington Polytechnic. Here, Head of School, Dave Davey, became another mentor to Alastair, guiding, challenging and supporting his team, which provided management education for companies small and large, across the breath of New Zealand.

Throughout Alastair's life, he has had a passion for learning and exploring. Over the years he became interested in the work of Tony Watkins, an Emeritus Professor and Town Planner in Auckland. Tony is an architect, author, educator and activist. He has been instrumental in developing local and global policy on sustainable development and architecture, and more broadly, sustainable life on the planet. His books include 'The Human House' and 'Piglet the Great of Karaka Bay'. Tony's work resonated with Alastair, thus strengthening his conviction in his own values, and how he was shaping his own life. Tony considered the transitory nature of material life, which also touched a chord with Alastair.

In 1974, Alastair and Jan bought a rural property and together with their three children they moved to Te Horo. Here on 18 acres they planted an organic orchard with a diversity of fruit trees, vegetables and a wide variety of herbs – self-sufficiency was a byword. After eight years with 'The Management Centre', destiny called, and 'The Parsonage Hill/Te Horo Vineyards' began its 17-year boutique winery life. In the years since Alastair relocated to Te Horo, he made a moral choice adopting a vegan plant-based way of being in the world, supporting an abolitionist vegan ethos.

This recent photograph of Alastair was taken for a life-size vegan banner, which also includes the story of his childhood visit to the freezing works with his father. Alastair, as a Gold Card holder, (a discount card issued to all New Zealand residents aged 65+ when they apply for New Zealand Superannuation), also features in the series of banners, to illustrate that older people, living on plant-based food 'can be dangerously' healthy and spare our animal family. Sea Otters of the West coast of the United States (pictured on his T shirt), were almost wiped out 100+ years ago by the fur trade. Thanks to conservation efforts, sea otters are now thriving on the Californian coast.

Alastair has spent years renovating his 135-year-old home in Te Horo, enjoying and employing the 'human house' philosophies developed through his friendship with Tony Watkins. This home 'with a mission', is a work in progress. It is being developed with wonderful support from his qualified builder buddy Chris, and Alastair's young and energetic son Campbell. Alastair has various roles in the project himself – 'visionary, site manager, worker to instructions' and 'the payer of bills'.

Alastair's 'Big Overseas Experience', which he commenced at the age of 60, has been purposeful and deeply connected– in his words 'to hear stories, meet people, locate places where scenes play out', and to 'fill his mind and camera with images'.

This photograph of Alastair was taken in the Eagle and Child pub in Oxford; in the very room where J.R.R. Tolkien and C.S. Lewis and friends met, "to wrestle with life, meaning and purpose and to discuss the books they were writing over a pint". In this pub, Alastair joined them in spirit and drank a loving toast to their memories and achievements. During this period in his life, Alastair has written five books which chronicle the adventures of 'The Motley Crew Family of Animals' – where animals are the heroes and humankind is the villain. Following in his Mum's footsteps, he travels 'low budget' and as a life member of the Youth Hostel Association enjoys meeting 'similarly minded explorers'. In his travels he has purposely set out to 'meet the locals' and investigate with his heart and mind the communities, the people and their lives. What he brought home were life experiences, photos and imaginative connections for the 'Motley Crew' adventures – not possessions. The Motley Crew adventures were primarily written for his family to enjoy; a synopsis of all five adventures can be seen on the Motley Crew's website https://motleycrewanimals.wordpress.com/

Alastair, who celebrates his 81st birthday this year, relishes life outdoors and is very active. He belongs to the local Kapiti Weekday Walkers group and enjoys hiking in the hills with 'can do' people, who like him, 'appreciate the beauty of the environment and the wonder of our earthly home'. He also likes riding his mountain bike; Folk Music at the Levin Club; Scottish Country Dancing and playing Bridge. His mantra is to "stay engaged and make things happen". Not surprisingly he has numerous projects on the go, one of which is writing more books. As a foundation member of the Otaki local Menzshed he says he "likes and appreciates the community focus and the freedom to just drop in for a cuppa, or work on your own or community projects". The Otaki Menzshed is "a bit unique" as it has several female members who actively participate in 'the life of the shed'.

Alastair is currently focusing on a legacy project for his three children and seven grandchildren. He is making them each a treasure chest with significant assistance from his friend Russell at the Otaki Menzshed. These treasure chests hold family heritage items that Alastair has personally found meaningful and valuable – hence his wish to share them with his whanau (family). The treasure chests, made from rough sawn macrocarpa (a New Zealand native tree), planed and gauged at the Menzshed, are an 'outworking of a yearning' to share 'life's meaning' connecting at least four generations in Alastair's family. When we talked, he said 'there are smooth and rough sides to the chest – this is symbolic, as our life journey is not always smooth, life has its ups and downs'. Each chest lid will be engraved with his child's or grandchild's name. Inside the legend reads 'Happy 21st' (or 50th for his children), with their birthdate, and, as in the photo, a heart is carved.

The exterior of one of the Treasure Chests

Inside one of the Treasure Chests

Each treasure chest will be lined with woven material, (as seen in the photo), or with screen-printed material from Alastair's Mum. In addition, physical remnants of the family's past whakapapa, (genealogy), proclaiming their identity, opening the connection to a wider family context, and linking the McAlpine (his mother's maiden name) and the Pain family to each other; the earth and all life. For example, there will be a file of sand from the Dalai Lama's 'Mandala of Compassion', which may be described as 'an out-picturing of love and compassion', that was brought to life by Buddhist monks in Whangarei. Mandalas are pictures, created, in intricate detail with granules of crushed coloured stone, by teams of monks over several weeks. It's a spiritual ritual. The pictures represent the cosmos, usually completed to focus the attention for meditation and spiritual guidance. The colours for the painting are usually made with naturally coloured sand, although corn meal, powdered roots and flower pollen is also used. When the sand mandala has been completed, the picture is swept up, the colours of the sand are intermingled, and the sand is released back into nature symbolising the transitory nature of life. It's a spiritual connection Alastair is gifting to his family.

This mandala, the Dalai Lama's, was created by the monks of the Jam Tse Dhargyey Ling, Tibetan Buddhist Meditation and Teaching Centre, in Kamo, Whangarei. Also included in the treasure chest will be a collection of books that Alastair has found particularly valuable on his life journey. These include:

- 'Memories Dreams Reflections', C.G. Jung's biography
- 'The God Delusion', by Richard Dawkins
- 'Women who run with the wolves' by Clarrisa Pinkola Estes
- 'Care of the Soul' by Thomas Moore
- 'Myths to Live By' by Joseph Campbell
- 'Science in the Soul' by Richard Dawkins.

All of these books provide powerful insights, stimulate the imagination and challenge preconceived mindsets. Alastair will also include personal copies of the five books he has written, chronicling the adventures of 'The Motley Crew Family of Animals'.

Alastair lives a very full and purposeful life. He is committed to abolitionist animal rights, and the idea that all of life is of 'One Being', and for him, being a vegan is a joy, not a sacrifice.

In closing, he shares this quote from Neil deGrasse Tyson that encapsulates the idea that all life is one being.

"The atoms of our bodies are traceable to stars that manufactured them in their cores and exploded these enriched ingredients across our galaxy, billions of years ago. For this reason, we are biologically connected to every other living thing in the world. We are chemically connected to all molecules on Earth. And we are atomically connected to all atoms in the universe. We are not figuratively, but literally stardust."

If you would like to chat about becoming a vegan, or sustaining a vegan diet and lifestyle, Alastair can be contacted at tehorowine@gmail.com

JEAN ST JOHN

Jean was born at the London Hospital in 1936 within the sound of Bow Bells referring to St Mary-Le-Bow Church (a historic church rebuilt after the Great Fire of 1666 by Sir Christopher Wren in the City of London). Jean is therefore a fully-fledged London Cockney. She was brought up in Islington which includes a significant area to the North, and now forms part of central London, but in wartime, times were tough, and Islington was not a highly sought-after area to live. There were extreme food shortages and most edible goods and other commodities such as clothing and coal were rationed. A period of intense bombing of London, known as the Blitz, began in 1940. During the bombing, which occurred-at all hours of the day and night, people took shelter wherever they could either fleeing to the Underground railway stations or to the Anderson shelters built at the end of the family's garden.

During the day, Jean's father worked as a wallpaper Silk Screen printer. At night he was an Air Raid Warden responsible for enforcing the 'blackout' in the borough to prevent enemy aircraft identifying their targets. In this role, he reported bombing incidents and worked closely with the Police and Fire Brigade to rescue survivors from their bombed homes and took care of the injured. Jean's mother remained home with the two children refusing to go to the shelters when the relentless bombing took place as she believed they were safer in their own home rather than in the streets and shelters.

Millions of children were evacuated to safer places during the war. Jean recalls boarding a coach with other children to be relocated elsewhere and then her Mother refusing to let them go taking them off the coach and back to home. Eventually, Jean and her brother Sam were evacuated to Ilkley Moor in the depths of Yorkshire, but recalls they were not happy times. In due course Jean's Mother travelled the long journey North to bring her children back to London.

Jean went to Sir Hugh Myddelton Secondary School and from there secured her first job as Junior Secretary to the Senior Reader with a prominent literary agency in Fleet Street in the City of London. She said she didn't have an interview for the role and acknowledges that this would not be the case today. The school was approached by the agency who were looking for a junior secretary and the Principal recommended Jean for the role. Jean said she feels so lucky to have been selected and in the course of her work had the opportunity to meet many famous authors and script writers, the likes of whom remain in the public eye to this day.

There was unprecedented change in post-war England. In the 1950's and early 1960s the population was coming to grips with the aftermath of war, and challenges involving reconstruction, political and social change. During this period, young skilled workers and their families were given the opportunity to emigrate to New Zealand, which offered them opportunities they could only dream of. Giving this opportunity long and very careful thought, Jean and her husband Tony decided to take the plunge and arrived in New Zealand during a very welcome heatwave in early 1961. The lovely suburb of Island Bay eventually became home to the family with Jean's three sons, Tim, Graham and Lloyd enjoying a wonderful beachside life. The family loved the lifestyle, became very close friends with other couples with young families who, like them, had emigrated from the United Kingdom (UK), leaving all their relatives behind to begin a new adventure in their lives. This group of friends became lifelong extended family with most of the families, festive and special occasions, for example birthdays, parties and weddings, celebrated together.

Over the years, Jean made several trips back to the United Kingdom to visit her parents in London taking the three children with her to meet their grandparents. She remembers spending six weeks in England, having been at sea for six weeks on the journey from New Zealand to England. They then boarded the ship for a further six weeks for the return journey – a hugely responsible task with the children being from the age of five years and under. It was around about this time that she started writing short stories as a hobby, often recording personal thoughts and specific events with family and friends. This is an activity Jean still pursues to this day.

Jean worked as a Secretary for the Wellington City Council. On retirement, with spare time on her hands, she gave some thought as to the next step. She had an idea – why not put an advertisement in the local paper volunteering as a Secretary? Within hours of the advertisement appearing, two gentlemen from the Horowhenua Branch of the Royal New Zealand Air Force Association, (RNZAFA), contacted Jean and immediately took her up on her offer. Jean carried out her voluntary duties in this capacity for the next 20 years with Tony her husband, happily becoming involved with any computer requirements necessary.

In her early 60's, Jean and Tony and their close friends, who all retired around the same time, formed a group called the SODS (Super annuitants Outing Days). Hilarious meetings took place every month and interesting outings were organised including an 'Adopt a Tree' day at Massey, mystery trips and general fun days out. Jean, as Secretary, kept a note of these outings and recorded a written summary of what they did when these outings took place. These notes were full of humour, so everyone looked forward to receiving a copy and to this day these notes still exist. The theme for the SODS' Millennium year 2000 get-together was 'Who Needs Mates'. For this especially important occasion everyone had to attend depicting a person whom they had admired during the past century. Tony presented himself as George Gershwin (inadvertently recognised as Popeye by the rest of the group), and Jean as a very unrecognisable Cleopatra. Jean recalls it as being hilarious as all present had to perform a skit on their chosen personality.

As time progressed, Tony's health declined and eventually he became a double amputee. The couple agreed that given Tony's health they needed to move out of their home. They subsequently chose to move to Otaki, 74 kilometres North of Wellington, close to the beach and where the people were friendly and there was so much to do. They loved their new home and became involved in the community, but sadly Tony passed away in 2012.

Jean, now 83 years of age, still lives in their Otaki home and manages the garden and household chores herself. She spends a great deal of time at the beach and swims both at the Otaki river and beach. She joined the local Kori Kaumatua Fitness Class seven years ago and attends these classes twice weekly. Jean says. 'it is so much fun with up to 50 others attending each session'. Two years ago, she and several friends from the exercise class were given the opportunity to stay behind after class to undertake Te Reo language classes together. Jean is immensely proud to be learning a new language and looks forward to continuing both classes with her friends in the future.

Jean, with like-minded friends, attends a small writing group which meets monthly to share their stories with each other. Over the years, she has accumulated quite a collection of her stories and has also written a children's book. As a member of Amicus (formerly Probus), she recently shared one of her stories at a meeting with her fellow members. The story is called 'A Release From Guilt'. It is a letter that she wrote to her Mother 37 years after her Mother had passed away. When Jean read the letter out loud, the group found it very moving. Jean explained that she found writing the letter to her Mother, whom she loved dearly, an opportunity to express her gratitude for the things she had taken for granted during the dramatic and difficult days of being brought up in war-torn London. As she explained, 'for everything you gain when you emigrate 12,000 miles away to another country for a better life for your family, guilt is the price to pay for those you love and leave behind'.

Jean is very close to her three sons and their families. A trip is being planned to Philadelphia in 2020. It is a place of great interest to Jean and she is eagerly looking forward to the forthcoming trip. Jean is a joy to share time with. She demonstrates that it is never too late to learn, to have aims and ambitions, to plan ahead, to enjoy new people and new experiences, and still make time to share experiences with family and friends.

Jean sitting on her darling Tony's memorial seat at Otaki Beach

MARGARET WILLIAMS

As a young woman Margaret worked as a Staff Instructor for Hoover, a leading manufacturer of large home appliances used for cleaning and washing. As a senior employee based in London, Margaret, who had learned French, Spanish and German at school, travelled around the United Kingdom (UK) and other European countries training people in the showrooms and their customers on how to use these appliances. In 1960, Hoover provided washing and cleaning equipment for the athlete's village at the Olympic Games held in Rome. It was a fabulous opportunity for Margaret and the team at Hoover to promote their products on the global stage whilst providing practical support for the teams competing in this major international event.

On arrival at the Olympic village the team from Hoover set up their equipment, and as they had free access to everything and everyone at the event, they quickly developed rapport with many of the athletes, trainers, coaches, managers and sponsors. New Zealand was represented at these games with a team of 37 competitors, who took part in 28 events across nine sports. Margaret met and became friends with Charlie Saunders, the Manager of the New Zealand team, and his wife Merle who were from Blenheim. Margaret recollects how exhausted the New Zealand hockey team were when she met them as they had been travelling for 10 days, so she and her co-worker Jean offered to do their washing for them so they could settle in and prepare for their events. Margaret's practical support was greatly appreciated and subsequently publicity photographs were taken of her with three members of the team, Warwick Dalton, Les Mills and Norman Reid, with a Hoover washing machine. Margaret treasures these photos to this day.

Margaret, Charlie and his wife Merle stayed in touch, and the following year (1961) Margaret decided to visit New Zealand. Charlie and Merle travelled up from their home in Blenheim to meet Margaret when she arrived in Wellington on the 'Southern Cross' passenger ship. Margaret stayed with the Saunders for six weeks and was then offered a job at Phillips Electrical. Television had only just been introduced in New Zealand, so they were a relatively new commodity for the general public. The job with Phillips gave her a chance to travel around New Zealand selling the concept.

Margaret enjoyed her new job in New Zealand and within a year she met and married her husband. The couple set up home and had two children, but unfortunately the marriage didn't last forever. As an independent woman she had always led a busy and active life. In 1978, Margaret, who was an only child, made the decision to return to England to care for her ageing parents who had retired to Lincolnshire while she had been away. Back in the UK, while caring for her children and parents, she took on several voluntary roles in the community.

When her parents died, Margaret bought a home in Louth, where she was employed as a youth worker. She also worked as a volunteer with Diabetes UK – a leading charity for people who, like herself, were living with diabetes. In Louth she met and became close friends with Greta, a Paediatric Consultant who did some contract work for the World Health Organisation. Greta's parents and grandparents had escaped from Russia during the uprising and she had been raised in Australia. One of Margaret's strengths was languages, and communication more generally. She had also travelled extensively and could quickly develop rapport with people from other cultures. The two like-minded women forged a friendship and when Greta was offered work in St. Petersburg in Russia to introduce the concept of volunteering in that country, she invited Margaret and two other volunteers to join her. This first volunteering project was aimed at educating General Practitioners, nurses and hospital staff on what volunteering is, how it works and the benefits for those who volunteer and the community. The project was funded by the World Health Organisation. By this time Margaret's children had grown up and flown the nest and she was thrilled to be able to contribute, and what's more, she learnt to speak some Russian. Margaret really enjoyed being able to share her skills and experience with others, and she and Greta have remained friends to this day.

As time passed Margaret's son David married, had a son and still lives in the UK. Her daughter Susan became a nurse with the British Army and later lived in Los Angeles for over 10 years, where Margaret visited her several times. Interestingly her daughter returned to New Zealand on her honeymoon and she and her husband set up home in Levin a few months later. Margaret retired aged 60 in the UK, which by this time had become a very densely populated country. Although the land mass is similar in size to New Zealand, with a population of more than 63 million people (according to the 2011 census), it seemed to Margaret that the infrastructure struggled to maintain them. Over the years Margaret had been back to New Zealand on numerous occasions to visit her friends and still had a sense of belonging there. Nine years ago, at 75 years of age, she transferred her pension and came back to New Zealand. She lives in Levin within walking distance of the town centre and in relatively close proximity to her daughter. She said she 'has never regretted it'.

Margaret calls herself a 'train nerd'. She was born near Kings Cross Station in London and learned all about the various trains and railway schedules from her Uncle Jack who was the station master for several years. Ever since then she has been a railway enthusiast. Now, as a retiree she has chosen to live near the main trunk line and enjoys being able to tell the time as the 'Capital Connection' passes through Levin to its destination. A keen gardener, Margaret joined the Garden Club and quickly developed friendships in the local community.

Margaret standing on the spot where she got married in a garden in Christchurch

Margaret joined the Horowhenua branch of Diabetes New Zealand and was on the committee for several years publicising information about this condition and supporting people from diagnosis onwards. She also joined Grey Power, an advocacy organisation in New Zealand that promotes the welfare and wellbeing of citizens in the 50 plus age group, and soon became a committee member. She is also on Grey Power's 'Health sub-committee', keeping members informed on health service provision. As she becomes aware of any health issues, she proactively meets and negotiates with the District Health Board to ensure quality health services are adequately provided for the Horowhenua community. Margaret represents Grey Power on Horowhenua District Council's 'Older Persons Network', and the 'Older Person's Network Community Wellbeing Committee'. As she is a walker, she represents pedestrians on Horizons Regional Council's 'Road Safety Committee'.

Over the years, in her free time, Margaret had two prime occupations – reading and writing. Despite an eyesight condition she has had since she was six years old, she is very well read, and takes a great interest in global and local current affairs. She is a committee member on 'Friends of the Library', a charitable group that supports the local library 'Te Takere' and has a significant collection of World War II books. Margaret also has accumulated a compendium of greeting cards as she is an ardent handwritten letter writer. She explains that 'everyone enjoys receiving a card or a letter from a friend or relative'. This form of connection lets people know that someone is not only thinking about you, but cares about you. Taking the time to write a letter 'takes time and is very personal'. To Margaret it is almost like having physical contact with another individual as it means so much to both parties; the person sending the letter and the person receiving it. Handwriting a letter seems to be a dying art in today's technological world of quick impersonal emails, which is a world that not everyone has access to. Margaret reminds us that writing a letter can bring so much joy and lighten someone's day. It's a practice we could all revitalise in our lives.

At the time of writing, Margaret aged 84, shows that staying connected can boost health and longevity as well as your enjoyment of life. How we pass our time in life, especially in later life really matters.

"In an age like ours, which is not given to letter-writing, we forget what an important part it used to play in people's lives". – Anatole Broyard

SHIRLEY AND TONY WELCH

Shirley and Tony grew up in Feilding, a small town in the Manawatu District of New Zealand and have known each other for most of their lives. They met in 1940, when they were five years old at Manchester Street School and were in the same class all the way through primary school. They both attended Feilding Agricultural High School, where Tony was sports minded rather than studying. Both Tony and Shirley were the youngest children in their families – Tony had three elder siblings and Shirley, was the youngest of seven. Shirley recalls that, as the baby of the family, everyone tried to bring her up, and there were always big things arranged for her to do or be. Growing up, Shirley was interested in gardening and flower arranging. Later she took up knitting, sewing, dressmaking, needlework and tapestry – hobbies that she has maintained throughout her life. She was also keen on roller skating and badminton. Her neighbours and family encouraged her to enter floral exhibits at the local flower shows, which she did. Ray, one of Shirley's twin brothers, had high aspirations for Shirley. He suggested she could play tennis (a sport he loved) at Wimbledon, or work at Kew Gardens in London or own a flower shop.

On leaving school Tony pursued an apprenticeship in the building trade. In 1952 Shirley was fortunate to be employed with the Horticultural staff at Massey University in Palmerston North where she assisted Miss Margaret O'Brien with floral art and the identification of plants. In this role Shirley worked in the glass house attending to the carnations and roses that were grown under glass. She also worked in the trial rose grounds for New Zealand and the lovely gardens surrounding the Mogenie Women's Hostel. Here she picked, soaked and bunched roses three days a week and sent them to florists in Palmerston North and Wellington. Late 1953, Shirley returned to Feilding to work in a pharmacy.

Both Shirley and Tony enjoyed being part of the Feilding's 4 C Club (Community Centre Co-education and Culture Club). They were also part of the Little Theatre, acting in many of the different plays and musical productions. In their teens, Tony and Shirley became members of the Committee for the Feilding High School Old Pupils Association where they helped organise the school reunions each year. They enjoyed each other's company, shared the same sense of humour and began dating. By this time Tony had acquired a 1927 Austin car, enabling the couple to attend the local and country dances in the neighbouring towns of Te Arakura, Ashurst and Marton.

On 6th January 1954, the Royal Civic Dinner Committee invited Shirley to be involved in the floral decorations for Queen Elizabeth's visit and dinner. This event was held at C. M. Ross Ltd., beautiful tearooms in Palmerston North. Naturally, she was delighted to be involved. Both Tony and Shirley were actively involved in the community in which they lived and helped raise funds to build Feilding Civic Centre. The major fundraising event was the Feilding queen carnival held in 1954 where 26,000 pounds was raised. Shirley was the Jaycee Queen, with the others being the Services, Sport and Country Queens. Shirley was awarded second place in the event which was held after four months of hard work organising concerts, dances and Gala days to raise the funds. Looking back Tony and Shirley said it was 'most enjoyable and quite exhausting'.

Feilding Queen Carnival Opening Ceremony
Mayor McClure, Margaret Knight, Ida Marshall, Helen Short, Shirley Cleland, Mayoress McClure

Jaycee Queen Shirley Cleland at the Mannequin Parade

Feilding's Civic Centre was constructed in the mid 1950's with the support of a volunteer labour force from the local community. The official opening of the Centre was held in February 1957.

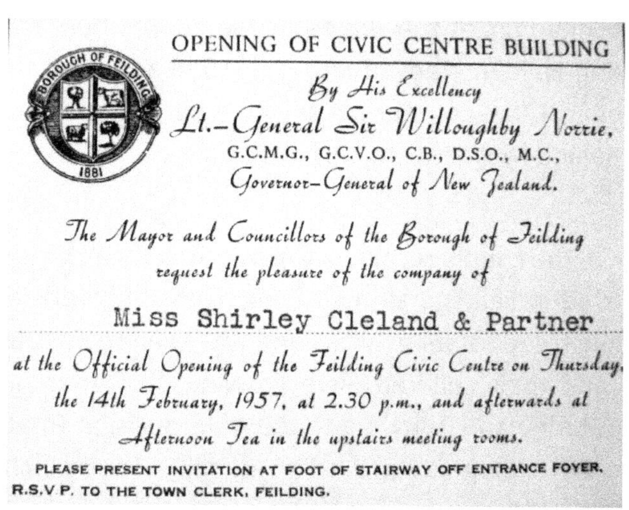

The same year Tony and Shirley married in Feilding.

Tony continued to work in the building trade and Shirley worked for a Dahlia specialist and his wife the florist. Whilst they took part in shared interests and family activities, they also encouraged one another to maintain their friendships with others, pursue their own hobbies and Tony was an active member of the Jaycees. The couple built their first home in Feilding, moved into it in 1958 and lived there for the next 12 years, during which time their two children Joanne and Megan were born.

In 1969, the couple recognised it was time for a change. They had lived in Feilding all their lives, Tony had worked in the building trade for many years and was keen to do something else, and their children were growing up. After talking it over, Shirley and Tony made the bold decision to sell their home in Feilding and move to Taranaki. They purchased a dairy (a small owner operated grocery store), in Okaiawa, a settlement 14 kilometres north-west of Hawera. The store was open six and a half days a week and the family lived directly behind it. From this location Tony also operated an owner operator 24-hour taxi business and drove the local school bus servicing the rural community. Despite their friends' concerns who said, 'oh, but you'll be together all the time', the couple enjoyed working together as a team and had always had a sense of 'we are in this together'.

The family became an integral part of this rural community for the next four years. One day, quite by chance, a friend told them about a new opportunity at the Kohitere Boys Training Centre in the Horowhenua, which operated under the social welfare system. Reflecting on his skills and experience Tony not only had a trade, he had strong personal qualities, a sense of community and could relate to people from all walks of life. The opportunity to work with troubled youth and help make a difference in their lives appealed to Tony. When a vacancy became available, he applied for a role as a Residential Social Worker at Kohitere, and following an interview was appointed to the job.

The Kohitere complex, located on the outskirts of Levin, was an open institution with no fences and gates. It was set up to rehabilitate young male offenders 14-17 years of age who were referred through the Department of Social Welfare. The residential programme was strongly focused on developing practical skills for the workplace. Practical experience in a variety of trades was offered under supervision (e.g. farming, forestry, carpentry and building, painting and mechanical trades). Secondary schooling and a wide variety of social, cultural and recreational activities such as sport, camping and kayaking were an integral part of the programme. At any one time there could be up to 100 young men on the premises, who came from all over New Zealand and from all walks of life.   In the 1970's Kohitere had a residential staff training school where the staff could attend either short or fully certificated training courses.

Shirley and Tony sold the dairy and the family moved into one of the houses provided for the residential staff in the same street as the Kohitere complex. The institution had a large number of staff and although he initially felt inexperienced in the role, Tony soon found he had a natural affinity for the work and could relate well to the residents. As time progressed, he took on more senior positions. As Tony was reasonably fit and ran every day, he facilitated an exercise programme for the residents and ran the cricket team in addition to his shift work. Tony really loved his job; it was a meaningful and often rewarding vocation. Over the next 17 years he worked with hundreds of teenagers whose lives, until then, had been quite challenging. He discovered that for some of the residents, life at Kohitere was a safe haven in comparison with what they had been accustomed to in the past. The experience provided the residents with an opportunity to take time out from their problematic circumstances, appreciate life from a different perspective, cultivate mutual respect and consider the choices an alternative lifestyle offered them in the future.

During these years Tony and Shirley's daughters, Joanne and Megan grew up in the Horowhenua and left home. Kohitere was a big part of their lives and the experience did them no harm. In fact, following her studies Megan became the first youngest female Residential Social Worker in New Zealand, and the first woman to work at the Hamilton Boys Home. Shirley worked in a local pharmacy. She also became the patron of the Horowhenua Rose Society and joined the Genealogy Society. Both Tony and Shirley were active members of the Methodist Church and in their spare time Tony played golf and Shirley played badminton. The couple had a caravan and together with their family travelled all over New Zealand during the holidays. They also enjoyed several overseas trips to Fiji, Norfolk Island and Australia.

In the later years, increasingly difficult residents were referred to Kohitere, but the institution was not designed, or resourced, to manage these situations, which in turn created stress for the staff and the residents. Tony's last year at

Kohitere was quite stressful. He began to experience health issues and had to take early retirement from his job, forfeiting the home that went with it.   Eventually he underwent open heart surgery

Tony and Shirley bought a property in Levin and moved into town. Recovering from his surgery Tony worked part-time on-call for a Toyota dealership delivering cars from one depot to another and undertook voluntary work for a while. Following 19 years' service at the pharmacy Shirley retired in 1999 aged 64. Over the years, the couple maintained contact with their family and friends in Feilding, and in 2007, the four Carnival Queens got together to again to celebrate Feilding's Civic Centre 50th birthday.

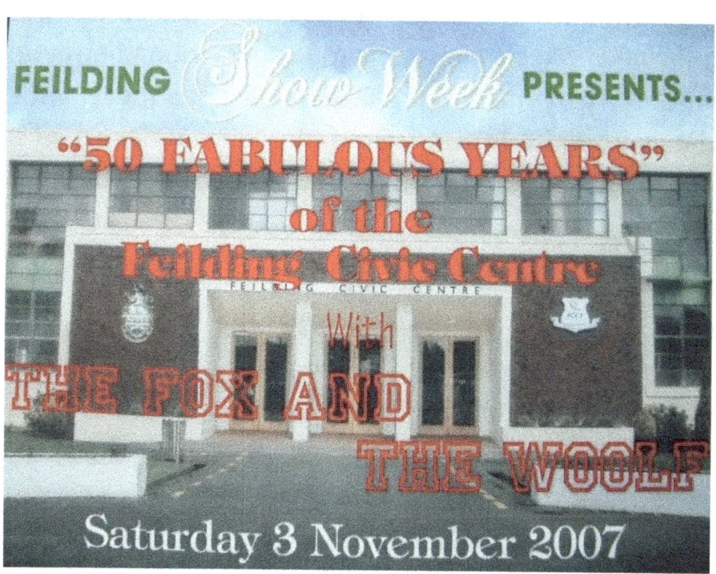

In retirement Tony and Shirley enjoy each other's company and their shared sense of humour as much as they ever did. They both enjoy walking, gardening - tending their beautiful

roses (80 hybrid trees and miniatures), and appreciate that 'as we get older, we must look ahead' and are therefore actively involved in the community. For more than 12 years they have been involved with the Levin Folk Club, which has played a longstanding part in New Zealand's folk music scene and a popular place for local and international artists to perform. The couple are both on the 'Thompson House Committee' that oversees a gracious old home in Levin's town centre. Built in the 1920's, this house has been set up as a cultural centre, popular with artists, craftspeople, clubs and community organisations for workshops, meetings and exhibitions. Shirley is a member of the Horowhenua 'Older Persons Network' set up to encourage collaborative conversation and information sharing to support positive ageing in the community. Tony plays 18 holes of golf twice a week with his friends. Throughout her life Shirley has meticulously kept a journal and is now writing her memoirs entitled 'Then There Were Seven'. She still meets with her friends from the Tapestry Group for lunch on a regular basis and belongs to various church groups.

At the time of writing Tony and Shirley, both 84 years young, have been happily married for 63 years. They enjoy a close relationship with their two children, three grandchildren and two great grandchildren. In their own words they 'love life together'.

Tony and Shirley at home

Tony is full of admiration for his 'amazing' wife who has stood beside him over the years through thick and thin. He has learned that "you have to respect and love yourself first, otherwise you can't give love to another". They have experienced tough times, including grappling serious health issues, but as Shirley says, "when you are in it, you can't run away and have to work through it". Tony and Shirley believe "a good marriage isn't about luck". This couple share the same values and sense of humour. They are also willing and able to discuss anything and everything with one another. They operate as a team with a sense of "we are in this together" - in essence, they are passionate about one another.

AFTERTHOUGHTS

It's been an honour to have met these individuals, and a privilege to be able to share their stories with you. These are not famous people - they are people from all walks of life, just like you and me. As you have seen, the diversity within this group of people, is truly amazing. Chronological age and the physiological aspects of ageing varied from person to person. In their fifties, sixties, seventies and eighties, they are single, have partners or are married or widowed – just like us. Regardless of their age and stage, these men and women are proactive and resilient. They choose to pursue activities that interest them to maintain their physical and mental health and wellbeing. All but three were eligible for government superannuation, but some individuals, had chosen not to retire from paid work. Several had started their own businesses in either their fifties, sixties or seventies. Others were busy undertaking voluntary work, actively contributing to their community in an unpaid capacity. A few were doing a combination of these things - because they want to - it's a conscious lifestyle choice. Age is irrelevant to these men and women, who are taking on new challenges, are learning new skills and are taking calculated risks.

All of these individuals, without exception, celebrate their experiences and achievements and live their lives on their own terms. They have made up their minds about how they want to spend their time and who they want to spend their time with. They pursue their passions, seek new opportunities, make big decisions, try new experiences, take on significant projects, are adventurous, invest in meaningful relationships, enjoy a good laugh, are connected to family and the community and plan and look forward to the future. These individuals recognise that their experiences and the lessons they learned along the way have shaped who they are and the choices they make. Their attitudes to life and their perspective on ageing is both insightful and inspirational. Their stories help dispel the assumptions and generalisations about how adults, from the intergenerational older population in our community, live their lives without regard for individual differences and unique circumstances.

I hope you have enjoyed reading about these men and women who are thriving in the second half of their lives. They have taken the time to reflect on their past experiences and the context in which they occurred. This exercise is not just a self-indulgent nostalgic trip down memory lane. Revisiting life events and the people associated can be a powerful experience – a journey of self-discovery. It's an opportunity to explore and reflect on the past and be mindfully aware of one's unique personality, gifts, strengths and achievements over the decades. It's an opportunity to appreciate the uplifting joyful times, create meaning from difficult and painful past experiences and gain insights from the thoughts, feelings and decisions associated with them. Reflection on our written stories helps to put our lives, our relationships and how we spend our time, into perspective. This learning experience also helps to propel us forward, think about the future and celebrate life on our own terms.

"Your story is the greatest legacy that you will leave to your friends. It's the longest-lasting legacy you will leave to your heirs" – Steve Saint

Increased longevity provides us with so many opportunities, a privilege denied to some of us. I encourage everyone to make the most of our extended lifespans. After all, life truly is a gift for us to enjoy, and, as an anonymous wise person once said.....

"The only limits in life are the ones you make"

THANK YOU

Thank you for reading *Celebrating Life On Our Own Terms*. I hope you enjoyed it. Reviews help other readers find books that may be of interest to them. I'd really appreciate it if you would take a couple of minutes to provide a review on this book, whether positive or negative.

By the same author

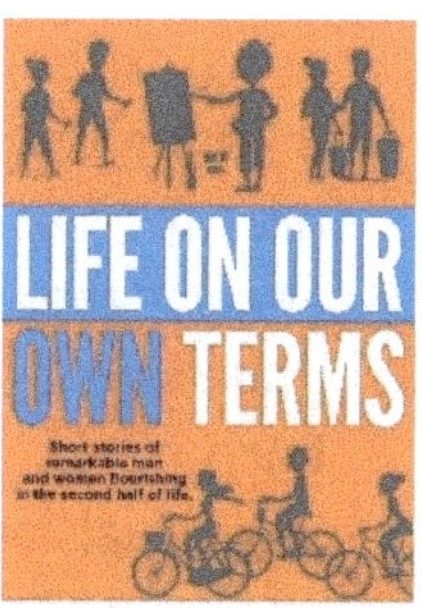

The first collection of stories in the *'Older and Bolder'* series

Available online from your favourite bookstores
ISBN: 978-0-473-50082-5 Paperback
ISBN: 978-0-473-50084-9 Kindle

Coming soon

Reimagining Retirement - Life After Work
Would you like to know when this book is available?
If so, email me to register your interest and be one of the
first to find out when it is released
kiaora@angelarobertson.nz

ABOUT THE AUTHOR

Dr Angela Robertson has over 30 years experiences as a professional learning and development practitioner, manager, coach, writer and speaker. Passionate about maximising potential, she encourages and supports individuals and teams to embrace and fully engage in the new and enriched experiences that change presents to enhance the quality of their lives, work and relationships.

Angela lives with her husband Bill on the beautiful Kapiti Coast in New Zealand.